Flavors of Sicily

Flavors of Sicily

FRESH AND VIBRANT RECIPES FROM A UNIQUE
MEDITERRANEAN ISLAND

URSULA FERRIGNO

WITH PHOTOGRAPHY BY David Munns

RYLAND PETERS & SMALL
LONDON • NEW YORK

Dedication

To Daddy, for showing me Sicily many years ago in a unique manner – a huge lunch conducted in a vineyard, with a grumpy driver and a flat tyre.

Senior Designer Toni Kay
Commissioning Editor Nathan Joyce
Picture Manager Christina Borsi
Head of Production Patricia Harrington
Art Director Leslie Harrington
Editorial Director Julia Charles
Publisher Cindy Richards

Food Stylist Emily Kydd
Prop Stylist Victoria Allen
Indexer Vanessa Bird

First published in the United Kingdom in 2016 by Ryland Peters & Small
20–21 Jockey's Fields
London WC1R 4BW
and
341 East 116th Street
New York NY 10029
www.rylandpeters.com

UK ISBN: 978-1-84975-706-5
US ISBN: 978-1-84975-734-8

10 9 8 7 6 5 4 3 2 1

Notes

• Both British (metric) and American (imperial plus US cups) are included in these recipes; however, it is important to work with one set of measurements and not alternate between the two within a recipe.

• All spoon measurements are level unless otherwise specified.

• All eggs are medium (UK) or large (US), unless specified as large, in which case US extra large should be used. Uncooked or partially cooked eggs should not be served to the very old, frail, young children, pregnant women or those with compromised immune systems.

• Ovens should be preheated to the specified temperatures. We recommend using an oven thermometer. If using a fan-assisted oven, adjust temperatures according to the manufacturer's instructions.

• When a recipe calls for the grated zest of citrus fruit, buy unwaxed fruit and wash well before using. If you can only find treated fruit, scrub well in warm soapy water before using.

Contents

Introduction

Sicily is an intriguing, beguiling place. Its prominent position in the Mediterranean has crowned it with an ancient and lasting importance and led to repeated conquests over the centuries, giving it an extraordinary cultural legacy. It has one of the world's best cuisines thanks to the complex influences and fusion of flavours left behind by the Greeks, Romans, Arabs, Normans and Spanish who have each occupied this fertile land.

My first visit to Sicily was an eye opener. I accompanied my father – who ran a fruit and vegetable business – on a business trip, taking the ferry from mainland Italy. And my first taste of Sicilian food was in the ferry cafeteria – arancini were heaped into tiny mounds, the shape of Mount Etna. They were, like the people I was soon to meet, warm, generous, unexpected and comforting. These rice morsels, probably stemming originally from Arabia, were stuffed with hidden ingredients. There were five varieties, which seemed to reflect a brief history of Sicilian invaders with every bite. The rice had been stuffed with bolognese, cheese, meat, tomatoes, spices and rolled into a hand-held snack. Moreish and totally delicious, they were a beautiful statement of what was to come.

As we approached the shores, the snow-capped Mount Etna commanded attention and respect, with smoke billowing against the bluest of blue skies. It's no surprise that the volcanic soil is special; intensely rich and fertile, and combined with the brilliant sunshine, the land produces ingredients that are so wonderful they speak for themselves.

The island's unique food is bright, earthy and suffused with the intensity of the Sicilian sun. Not surprisingly, many of the typical dishes are made with fish and seafood. Cream and butter are rarely used and instead, juicy tomatoes or the island's own fragrant olive oil are substituted. Sheep's milk ricotta is another staple ingredient, as are black and green olives, wild fennel (which grows all over the hills) and the cultivated citrus fruits that are used in almost everything, from salads to desserts.

In the chapters that follow, you'll discover authentic recipes for the best food Sicily has to offer, starting with antipasti. Choose from Arancini di Riso (risotto croquettes) or Gustoso Olive Nero (olive relish). Vibrant salads such as Insalata di Orangio di Torocci (blood orange and red onion salad) are perfect for summer eating, as are the light soups and pasta dishes including Fogie di Zucchine con Pomodoro Fresche e Pastina (courgette/zucchini leaf and fresh tomato soup) or Pasta Picchi Pacchi (spaghetti with tomato and almond sauce). Delicious meat and fish recipes include Sardine a Beccafico (stuffed sardines) and Abbacchio alla Cacciatovia (pan-fried spring lamb with herbs and anchovy sauce). There are traditional breads, such as Pane Rimacinati (semolina mountain bread). Sicilians notoriously have a sweet tooth and are among the best dessert-makers in Italy. Indulge in Gelato al Pistachio (pistachio ice cream), Cannoli (pastry tubes filled with sweetened ricotta) and possibly Sicily's most famous export, Cassata.

Appetizers

Antipasti

Fried chickpeas with herbs

Ceci fritti con salvia e origano

This very simple treatment of chickpeas – which are abundant in Sicily – has its roots firmly anchored in North Africa. It's a popular street food, often eaten as a 'merenda' or afternoon snack, and also commonly served at 'Sagre' – festivals to celebrate the season of a particular ingredient. It's a welcome change from peanuts and crisps as an aperitivo, but also works in a salad.

200 g/1 cup plus 2 tablespoons dried chickpeas, soaked in water overnight with 2 bay leaves, 2 garlic cloves and a handful of parsley

olive oil or groundnut oil, for frying

a handful of rosemary needles

a handful of sage leaves, finely chopped

a handful of oregano leaves, finely chopped

1½ teaspoons fennel seeds

crushed sea salt, for sprinkling

finely grated zest of 1 unwaxed lemon

Serves 8

Drain the chickpeas and discard the soaking water, but keep the garlic and bay leaves.

Add the chickpeas, garlic and bay leaves to a saucepan filled with cold water. Bring to the boil and boil rapidly for 10 minutes. Reduce the heat and continue cooking for 20 minutes until the chickpeas are tender. Strain and place on a dry, clean dish towel and pat to remove excess moisture.

Heat the oil in a large frying pan/skillet set over medium heat and add a quarter of the chickpeas. Shallow-fry for 5 minutes. Add a quarter of the herbs and a quarter of the fennel seeds and cook for 3 minutes until fragrant. Remove with a slotted spoon and drain on paper towels. Repeat with the remaining ingredients in batches.

Transfer to a bowl and add sea salt to taste. Mix well and serve with the zest of the lemon.

Very tasty olive relish

Gustoso olive nero

300 g/2½ cups very tasty black olives (e.g. Gaeta), stoned/pitted

a generous handful of flat-leaf parsley leaves

2 garlic cloves, peeled

leaves stripped from 7–8 lemon thyme sprigs

6 fennel seeds (optional)

finely grated zest of 1 unwaxed lemon

about 3 tablespoons extra virgin olive oil

sea salt and freshly ground black pepper

Makes about 250 g/1 cup

I have been experimenting with this relish after my recent trip to Sicily and I think this recipe is as close to the version I enjoyed at Mandello beach. Serve on sourdough, or on one of the breads to be found on pages 112–125. Good bread is vital. Like great oil that breathes life into a dish, great bread elevates a dish to another level.

Combine all the ingredients together in a food processor and blend to a coarse texture.

Use immediately on toasted bread.

Fried vegetables with tomato sauce

Fritto misto con sugo di pomodoro

Fritto misto, or mixed fried food, is found mainly in Sicily. My grandmother, who comes from Minori on the Amalfi coast, cooks a version that includes Parmesan cheese in the batter, which is very good. Fritto misto consists of small morsels of vegetables in batter or breadcrumbs, which are deep fried and eaten straight away. Courgette/zucchini flowers may be included. The inclusion of chilli/chile and cloves in the tomato sauce illustrates the Arab influence on this dish.

olive oil, for deep frying

Italian '00' flour, for dusting

1 kg/2¼ lbs. mixed vegetables, e.g. (bell) peppers, aubergine/eggplant, asparagus, courgettes/zucchini, cut into 5-cm/2-inch strips

TOMATO SAUCE

2 tablespoons olive oil

2 shallots, finely chopped

2 garlic cloves, finely chopped

500 g/3 cups ripe tomatoes, chopped

3 teaspoons crushed dried chilli/chile (peperoncino)

2 cloves

sea salt and freshly ground black pepper

tomato purée/paste, to taste (optional)

a handful of flat-leaf parsley, finely chopped (optional)

BATTER

300 ml/1¼ cups milk

1 yolk (from UK medium/US large egg)

½ teaspoon sea salt

125 g/1 scant cup Italian '00' flour

½ teaspoon baking powder

Serves 4–6

To make the sauce, heat the oil in a medium-sized saucepan and cook the shallots for about 4 minutes over medium heat, until golden. Add the garlic and cook until soft. Add the tomato, chilli/chile, cloves and salt and pepper. Simmer gently for 20 minutes until thick and pulpy. Set aside, picking out the cloves (if you want to increase the colour to be a more vibrant red, add a little tomato purée/paste and continue cooking for 12 more minutes).

To make the batter, whisk together the milk, egg yolk and salt in a large bowl for about 3 minutes, or until smooth. Sift the flour into the bowl with the baking powder, and whisk together.

Heat 4 cm/1½ inches of olive oil in a deep frying pan/skillet. Spread a little flour on a plate. Dip the vegetable pieces one at a time into the flour and then in the batter to coat. Carefully drop into the oil in batches and cook for about 2 minutes, until golden. Drain well on paper towels.

Stir the parsley into the sauce, if using, and serve alongside the warm fritto misto.

Panelle

Panelle

This recipe is quite possibly the simplest in this book in terms of ingredients, but it truly fascinates me. For one, it has so many different names. In the south of France it is called socca; on the Ligurian coast of northern Italy, panisse, and in Tuscany, cecina or farinatta. All of them use chickpea/gram flour, but all with slightly different treatments. I find chickpea/gram flour extremely tasty and consider it a vital store cupboard ingredient. It can also be used to coat vegetables, meat and fish, and forms a crispy coating called panellina. During the research for this book, my daughter Antonia and I enjoyed a wonderful panelle in a restaurant called Buatta in Palermo. Traditionally it is served in a sesame-seed-coated bun with a squeeze of lemon. The friggitoria (fry shops) all over the city of Palermo sell this wonderful street food.

300 g/2¼ cups chickpea/gram flour

750 ml/3 cups water

1 teaspoon sea salt, plus extra to serve

freshly ground black pepper, to taste

a generous handful of flat-leaf parsley, freshly chopped

olive oil or groundnut oil, for deep frying

lemon wedges, to serve

Makes 8–12

Place the flour in the bottom of a medium-sized saucepan. Gradually add the water, stirring with a whisk the whole time until all the water has been used.

Place the saucepan over medium heat. Stir constantly. After 20 minutes, add the seasoning and parsley and continue to cook, stirring well, until the mixture pulls away from the sides of the pan, approximately 30 minutes.

Remove the pan from the heat and pour the mixture onto oiled baking sheets. Roll it flat with an oiled rolling pin and then leave to set for 45–60 minutes.

Cut the dough into 4 x 4-cm/1½ x 1½-inch pieces. Heat the oil in a frying pan/skillet.

Fry the dough pieces until golden, turning once. Serve immediately with a little extra sea salt on top and lemon wedges to the side.

Sicilian potato croquettes

Cazzilli o crocche di patate

The Sicilian dialect word 'cazzilli' (little penises) was jestingly given to these crispy croquettes on account of their shape. Friggitoria (fry shops) all over Palermo sell this super finger food in many different guises.

4 medium-sized (all the same size is preferable) old potatoes (i.e. King Edward, Desiree, Pentland Crown, Maris Piper, Rooster), cleaned

½ teaspoon nutmeg

75 g/5 tablespoons unsalted butter

a generous handful of flat-leaf parsley, freshly chopped

2 UK large/US extra large eggs, beaten

150 g/1¼ cups dried breadcrumbs

olive oil or groundnut oil, for deep frying

sea salt and freshly ground black pepper

Serves 4-6

Place the potatoes in a medium-sized saucepan of boiling water. Keep the potatoes cooking but not boiling (boiling will encourage the skins to burst). Cook for about 15 minutes, or until tender.

When the potatoes are tender, drain and leave to cool. Peel away the skins and press the potatoes through a ricer or food mill into a bowl. Don't use a food processor as this will develop the starch too much.

Add the salt, pepper, nutmeg, butter and parsley. Mix well and form into 10 x 7.5-cm/4 x 3-inch pieces. Roll into smaller rods (fork-friendly, size-wise).

Dip the rods into the beaten egg and then the breadcrumbs. Place on a parchment-lined tray and chill in the refrigerator for 30 minutes.

Heat the oil and fry in batches until golden. Drain on paper towels and sprinkle over some more salt if desired. Serve hot.

Fried courgette flowers

Frittelle di fiori di zucca

Unfortunately, my nonna wasn't keen to share her secret recipe for zucchini flower fritters. Whenever I ask her, she always shrugs her shoulders and says: 'It's luck!' I really hope you will enjoy my version. Some fabulous vegetable shops will sell the flowers in the summer but the best come from your very own plot. Be sure to keep them fresh in iced water before you cook them as they deteriorate very quickly.

7 g/1¼ teaspoons fresh yeast
(or 1 teaspoon dried/active dry yeast)

450 ml/1¾ cups warm water (37°C/99°F)

250 g/2 cups Italian '00' flour, sifted

2 tablespoons olive oil

groundnut oil, for frying

24 large courgette/zucchini flowers

a handful of flat-leaf parsley, freshly chopped

lemon quarters, to serve

sea salt and freshly ground black pepper

Serves 4-6

Dissolve the fresh yeast in a little of the water and set aside for 10 minutes. If using dried yeast, mix with the flour.

Mix the flour, water, oil, yeast mixture and salt and pepper well, using a whisk to beat out any lumps. Cover and leave to become bubbly for 45–60 minutes. Stir the bubbles in the batter.

Heat 8 cm/3 inches of groundnut oil in a deep pan. Remove the stamens from the courgette/zucchini flowers. Dip the flowers one at a time into the batter and shake off the excess.

Place one at a time in the oil, frying 4 at a time until golden, turning once. Remove with a slotted spoon and drain on paper towels, then sprinkle with parsley and salt. Serve straight away with lemon quarters.

Filled risotto croquettes

Arancini di riso

When you're food shopping in Sicily, everywhere you turn you will see arancini. They come in a multitude of sizes and with a wide variety of fillings. At the beach they seem to be quite large to match one's appetite. I have to confess that these cheese and ham ones with a splash of tomato sauce are my favourite, but even just herb and mozzarella is delicious. My family like theirs filled with meat sauce (ragù), but I recommend you experiment to find your own favourite.

250 g/1⅓ cups Arborio rice

a generous pinch of saffron strands

100 g/1⅓ cups freshly grated Pecorino cheese

100 g/3½ oz. young Pecorino cheese, cut into cubes

100 g/3½ oz. cooked ham, cut into cubes

100 g/3½ oz. passata/strained tomatoes, mixed with 2 crushed garlic cloves

a handful of flat-leaf parsley, freshly chopped

3 tablespoons Italian '00' flour

2 UK large/US extra large eggs, lightly beaten

150 g/1¼ cups dried breadcrumbs

olive oil or groundnut oil, for frying

sea salt and freshly ground black pepper

Makes 8–12

Cook the rice in salted water for approximately 10 minutes. Add the saffron and continue to cook for 8 more minutes until sticky. Drain and place the rice onto baking parchment-lined baking sheets, spreading the rice out to a thickness of 1 cm/½ inch.

Place a 6-cm/2½-inch round cutter or a tumbler over the surface of the rice to create individual portions of rice. Allow the rice to cool.

Place the grated cheese, cubed cheese, ham, 1 teaspoon of the passata/strained tomatoes and some parsley on each of the rice rounds. Season well.

Using a palette knife, lift the rounds off the baking sheets and form them into balls, carefully sealing in the filling. I place the round in the palm of my hand like a nest and squeeze gently to seal.

Dip the rounds in the flour, egg and breadcrumbs and deep fry until golden in plenty of oil. Lift out of the oil and drain on paper towels. Arancini are best served warm.

Fried gnocchi with salami

Gnocco fritto con salumi

I feel so very lucky to have spent 18 wonderful years teaching at La Cucina Caldesi in Marylebone, London and hope to enjoy another 18 years. I adore working with Italians – we are all so opinionated about food, but we are a very jolly, happy team. This recipe is my adaptation of Gregorio Piazza's; he's the Head Chef at the Caldesi in Campagna restaurant that Giancarlo and Katie Caldesi own in Bray, Berkshire. Like so many Sicilian antipasti, it is fried. You can vary the toppings, but keep them light and tasty.

160 ml/⅔ cup whole milk

7 g/1¼ teaspoons fresh yeast

350 g/2¾ cups Italian '00' flour

35 g/2 tablespoons unsalted butter, grated

1 teaspoon salt

2 teaspoons finely chopped fresh rosemary

semolina, for dusting

groundnut oil, for frying

selection of antipasti, such as salami, prosciutto, shaved Parmesan cheese and artichokes in oil, to serve

sea salt and freshly ground black pepper

Serves 4-6

Heat the milk gently until it reaches 37°C/99°F. Dissolve the yeast in the milk.

In a bowl, combine the flour, butter, salt, rosemary and milk mixture and mix well.

Turn out onto a floured board and knead until smooth, approximately 10 minutes. Transfer to an oiled bowl and leave to rise until it has doubled in size, approximately 1 hour.

Turn the dough onto a floured work surface and re-knead. Divide the dough into 4 equal pieces and feed through a pasta machine, starting with the #1 setting (the thickest setting) and working your way through to the thinnest setting, usually #6.

You should have 4 long strips of dough. Cut the dough with a pastry wheel (one with fluted edges) into 6-cm/2½-inch squares. Place the squares onto trays dusted with semolina, cover and leave for 1 hour.

Heat a generous quantity of oil in a large frying pan/skillet and fry the gnocchi in batches, turning once. This should take approximately 3 minutes. Drain on paper towels.

Serve with a selection of antipasti, such as cured meats, cheese and artichokes and season with salt and pepper.

Potato and ricotta balls

Polpette di patata e ricotta

The Sicilian love of potatoes is well documented. The fertile soil from Etna gives the potatoes grown there golden flesh and a very particular flavour. This recipe is extremely child-friendly as they love to discover the ricotta in the middle. I urge you to try it with other ingredients – ham, olives and onions are all good.

500 g/1 lb. 2 oz. old potatoes, scrubbed

2 UK large/US extra large eggs, plus 2 extra egg yolks

125 g/1½ cups freshly grated Parmesan cheese

1 teaspoon freshly grated nutmeg

a generous handful of flat-leaf parsley, freshly chopped

225 g/8 oz. ricotta cheese

100 g/1¼ cups dried breadcrumbs

olive oil, for frying (optional)

sea salt and freshly ground black pepper

Serves 8

Boil the potatoes in their skins, then peel and mash in a ricer. Add the two egg yolks and the Parmesan cheese, salt, pepper, nutmeg and parsley and mix well.

In a separate bowl, mash the ricotta and season well.

Beat the whole eggs in a bowl. Place the breadcrumbs in a separate bowl.

Make little nests of the potato mixture in your palms and fill up the hollows with a spoonful of ricotta. Seal the mixture to form a ball (the balls should be golf-ball sized). Continue to make more balls until all the mixture is completely used.

Dip each ball first into the beaten egg and then the breadcrumbs.

You can either fry the polpette until golden in olive oil or bake them in an oven preheated to 200°C (400°F) Gas 6 for 15 minutes until golden brown. Serve warm or cold. They are excellent for picnics and family gatherings.

Pan-fried provolone with olive oil

Provolone con olio do'livia

4 tablespoons olive oil, for frying

2 garlic cloves, crushed

700 g/1½ lbs. provolone cheese, cut into 2.5 x 1-cm/1 x ½-inch strips

4 tablespoons white wine vinegar or a little balsamic vinegar

4 teaspoons freshly chopped oregano

good-quality extra virgin olive oil, to serve

wonderful bread to mop up the juices

Serves 4

Provolone is a delicious southern Italian cheese made by first boiling cow's milk curds and then soaking the curds in brine. Sicilians are blessed with many varieties of provolone: dolce – a mild version aged for 2–3 months; piccante – sharp and spicy and aged for up to 1 year; and affumicato – lightly smoked for 1 week and then aged for 3–4 months. Please use good-quality ingredients for this recipe – it is such a simple recipe and benefits from a wonderful provolone. This dish can be made really quickly for an impromptu gathering.

Heat the olive oil in a large frying pan/skillet set over low heat. Sauté the garlic until coloured and then discard. Add the cheese, arranging it in a single layer. Cook for 3–4 minutes on each side, without allowing the cheese to burn. Transfer to a serving plate.

Pour over the vinegar and sprinkle with oregano. Serve immediately with a little good oil on top and some great bread.

Facciamoci un aperitivo!

Somewhere between 7pm and 9pm, before most Sicilians enjoy their evening meal, there come the golden hours which are filled with the long-cherished, authentic Italian tradition of aperitivo. A chance to unwind, socialise and share drinks and tapas-style light bites as dinner approaches. Aperitivo is a quintessentially Italian concept which is not solely focused on the food, or the drink or even the place, but steeped in the spirit of an Italian passion for socially connecting with family and friends.

OPPOSITE TOP LEFT
Olives and grissini are the perfect accompaniments to early evening drinks.

OPPOSITE TOP CENTRE
As daylight fades, the open-air restaurants and bars begin to fill up.

OPPOSITE TOP RIGHT
Campari can either be diluted with soda water or fruit juice, or used in cocktails such as the classic Negroni, where it is mixed with equal measures of gin and vermouth.

OPPOSITE Early evening in Siracusa and friends begin to gather for aperitivo.

Aperitivo is the name for both the social and tasty ritual of going out for a pre-dinner drink, as well as the sort of drink that you would probably have at such a ritual. It offers a moment of relaxation at the end of a day where you can allow yourself the pleasure of conversation paired with, like most good things in Italy, the added pleasure of delicious food.

The exact origins of the Italian aperitivo are hard to pinpoint. It has been said that the concept was started in Torino in 1786 by the creator of the vermouth liquor, Antonio Benedetto Carpano. A cunning marketing ploy perhaps but it is also been reported that in the 1860s, Gaspare Campari moved to Milan, where he opened a café and served his home-brewed invention, the Campari liquor. When mixed with soda and vermouth, this drink came to be known as the Americano and these bitter mixes were typically served alongside complimentary salty snacks. What matters most is that the tradition goes back hundreds of years and has continued throughout the centuries, with peaks in the 1920s when the concept enjoyed widespread popularity, again in the 1960s when it became part of fashionable culture and today, when the simple aperitivo still plays an important role in Italian social life. The success of the fast, easy, inexpensive and informal pairing of a drink and a bite to eat is sure to be enjoyed for hundreds of years to come.

Aperitivo comes from the Latin verb 'aperire' meaning 'to open' or stimulate your appetite and tease your tastebuds. In Italian, the charming expression, 'l'appetito vien mangiando' translates as 'appetite comes when you eat' – a truly Italian and wonderfully romantic notion about our longing for food.

To start with the drinks, wine is (of course) always an acceptable aperitivi but there are certain classic beverages which are equally thought to help kickstart your digestion and perhaps more suited to these happy Italian hours. They're usually refreshingly light and dry or even bitter rather than sweet – things like prosecco, vermouth, Campari or Aperol. In the beginning these were often served straight up or on the rocks, but now more commonly they are mixed to create classic spritzes and cocktails such as Negroni and Americano. Their non-alcoholic counterparts include drinks such as Sanbitter (bianco or rosso) and Crodino, bittersweet, slightly medicinal tasting soft drinks.

Looking back to the very start of the tradition, a small, complimentary antipasto offering of nuts, olives, perhaps some grissini, cheese or salumi, may have and may still accompany your drink. The food you are served depends on the establishment, but it is certain that as the tradition has grown, so has the trend for more elaborate, stylish and regional nibbles which are well worth seeking out, from awe-inspiring pastas, sensational seafood, mini arancini, pizzette, crostini, a showcase of fresh local vegetables and vibrant salads. The key is sharing, so expect small plates or larger platters to enjoy.

And, a note of restraint – although it wouldn't be hard to make a meal of some of the carefully chosen, quality dishes available, that would be to miss the point and fail to give the food the respect which Italians know it deserves. By delicately grazing and savouring just a little something, Italians believe that it will encourage you to feel hungry, and simply act as a preview to the delights of dinner which is still to come. Aperitivo is only the start...

Asparagus, provolone and mint skewers

Asparagi e provolone con menti spiedini

As I am writing this recipe, the asparagus season is in full swing. Each year I look at the pathetic amount in my plot and sigh – ever hopeful that a bumper crop will establish itself. Thankfully, our very generous neighbour steps in to provide us with armfuls each year. I enjoyed this colourful, tasty dish many years ago in Cefalu in northern Sicily with my mother.

24 even lengths of asparagus, trimmed to 7.5-cm/3-inch lengths

400 g/14 oz. provolone (use provolone affumicato if you like the smoked flavour)

6 tablespoons olive oil

good-quality extra virgin olive oil, for drizzling

a generous handful of fresh mint leaves

grated zest and freshly squeezed juice of 2 unwaxed lemons

sea salt and freshly ground black pepper

Serves 4

Blanch the asparagus in boiling water for 1 minute, then refresh in cold water.

Cut the provolone cheese lengthways into at least 12 pieces, about the same size as the asparagus.

Thread the asparagus and cheese onto wooden skewers. I usually skewer 2 asparagus pieces for each piece of cheese, so that every skewer contains 3 pieces of cheese and 6 asparagus lengths.

Heat a grill/broiler pan and brush olive oil over the skewers. Chargrill, turning once, until the cheese is golden.

Place on a platter and anoint with good-quality oil, mint leaves, lemon juice, zest, salt and pepper.

Salads and stuffed vegetables

Insalate

Onions baked in Marsala

Cipolle al forno alla Marsala

I was teaching a super group of students at Suffolk Food Hall one evening, and two of them commented on the oil I was using for a particular recipe, so I explained in detail why I had chosen it. A firm friendship and tremendous respect has evolved from this encounter with Will and Val. They have a family farm between Marsala and Trapani in western Sicily and make the most wonderful olive oil, called Racalia. This recipe is for them. Please use dry Marsala or dry sherry.

8 red onions

16 whole cloves

a handful of fresh thyme

3 fresh bay leaves

150 ml/⅔ cup dry Marsala or dry sherry

3 tablespoons Racalia extra virgin olive oil

sea salt and freshly ground black pepper

Serves 4-6

Preheat the oven to 180°C (350°F) Gas 4.

Cut the onions in half and stud each half with cloves.

Arrange in a single layer on a baking dish and add water to reach halfway up the onions. Sprinkle over the thyme sprigs and bay leaves.

Cover with foil and bake for 30 minutes in the preheated oven. The onions should be tender and the water should have evaporated – this will very much depend on the size of your onions, and their freshness etc. so keep checking that the onions are not drying out.

Remove the onions from the oven and remove the cloves. Pour over the Marsala and bake for another 20 minutes, uncovered.

Season with salt and pepper and anoint with fine oil. Serve on their own, with other vegetables as antipasti or to accompany meats.

Red peppers stuffed with fennel

Peperoni con finocchio

This colourful vegetable dish is very easy to prepare and will wow your veggie friends. I first encountered a version of it in Messina and subsequently in Catania too. It can be made a day ahead and reheated.

4 tablespoons olive oil

4 fennel bulbs

4 large rectangular sweet red (bell) peppers

2 onions, finely chopped

3 garlic cloves, finely chopped

200 g/7 oz. ricotta

80 g/¾ cup pistachio nuts, shelled and finely chopped

200 g/7 oz. passata/strained tomatoes

1 tablespoon tomato purée/paste

a handful of fresh flat-leaf parsley, finely chopped

a pinch of crushed dried chilli/chile (peperoncino)

fennel fronds, to garnish

sea salt and freshly ground black pepper

Serves 3–4

Preheat the oven to 180°C (350°F) Gas 4. Grease a wide baking dish with 1 tablespoon of the olive oil.

Halve the fennel bulbs lengthways and trim them, discarding the woody cores and reserving the leafy fronds.

Blanch the bulb halves for 8 minutes in a saucepan of boiling water. Drain and pat dry. Halve the (bell) peppers lengthways and remove the pith and the seeds.

Heat 2 tablespoons of the olive oil in a frying pan/skillet. Sauté the onions and then add the garlic.

Transfer the onions and garlic to a large bowl and add the ricotta. Season with salt and pepper and add the pistachio nuts. Place 3–4 spoonfuls of the mixture in each of the (bell) pepper halves. Place the fennel on top so that it sits on the cheese mixture. Add more mixture around the edges of each, to fill.

Transfer the (bell) peppers filled with cheese and fennel to the baking dish. Mix the passata/strained tomatoes and tomato purée/paste and season with parsley. Pour around the stuffed (bell) peppers. Drizzle the remaining oil on top of the peppers, and sprinkle with a pinch of peperoncino.

Cover with foil and bake for 30 minutes in the preheated oven until golden brown and bubbling. Serve garnished with fennel fronds.

Sweet and sour pumpkin

Zucca in agrodolce di catania

This is a typical Sicilian dish from Catania using sweet spice in a savoury context. Many Sicilian recipes utilize a combination of spices, nuts and dried fruits – a legacy of the island's Byzantine past. I adore pumpkin and I find it so versatile. Pumpkin's yellow-orange flesh is rich in beta-carotene (which the body converts into Vitamin A). If you save the seeds, you can dry them in a low oven and eat them as a snack. They are full of zinc.

1 kg/2¼ lbs. pumpkin, peeled and deseeded

5 tablespoons olive oil

2 garlic cloves, peeled and left whole

1 tablespoon caster/superfine sugar

a generous handful of mint leaves, freshly chopped, stems discarded

1 teaspoon ground cinnamon

1 tablespoon white wine vinegar

2 tablespoons good-quality extra virgin olive oil, for drizzling

sea salt and freshly ground black pepper

Serves 4

Cut the pumpkin flesh into slices, roughly 1 cm/½ inch thick.

Heat the olive oil in a frying pan/skillet over medium heat. When hot, add the pumpkin and whole garlic cloves. Discard the garlic as soon as it colours.

When the pumpkin slices are fried (you may have to do this in batches), place them all back together in the pan and drain the superfluous oil. Take off the heat.

Dredge with the sugar, mint and cinnamon. Mix well, then pour the vinegar over the top. Add salt and pepper to taste. Cover with a lid and leave to infuse.

Serve warm or cold, anointed with good extra virgin olive oil.

Orange and red onion salad

Insalata di orangio di tarocchi

The blood orange is one of Sicily's most famous exports. They are strongly fragrant with brilliant red peel and pulp. They come into season in January when our palate needs cheering up, and extra vitamins are most needed. The deliciously zingy tarocchi is widely used in salads, frozen ice cream desserts and sorbet. This salad is unashamedly simple and works well with small sweet oranges when blood oranges are sadly out of season.

4 blood oranges or other small sweet oranges

1 small red onion, cut into very thin rings

a handful of flat-leaf parsley, freshly chopped, stems discarded

4 tablespoons wonderful Sicilian extra virgin olive oil, or if you can't find it, any good-quality fresh, green olive oil

sea salt and freshly ground black pepper

Serves 4

Peel the oranges and remove the pith. Cut horizontally into thin slices and put in a bowl.

Add the rings of onion to the bowl with the oranges. Add the oil and half of the parsley, season with salt and pepper and toss until all the ingredients are well coated.

Arrange the oranges and rings of onion on a platter. Drizzle with the oil left in the bowl. Sprinkle with the remaining parsley and serve.

Spinach and broccoli caponata

Caponata di verdure

Most people will be familiar with the more well-known aubergine/eggplant caponata. When I stumbled across this dish in Palermo, however, I was so thrilled. Although an ancient dish, this is so in keeping with the green revolution that we are witnessing. I can say that there is quite simply no finer way of enjoying greens. Leftovers can be enjoyed cold the next day and taste so good for the extra marinating time. Mop up the juices with some good bread.

200 g/3½ cups Swiss chard, chopped

200 g/3½ cups spinach, chopped

125 g/4½ oz. tenderstem broccoli/broccolini, chopped

3 ribs/sticks celery (the whiter the better), chopped

200 g/3½ cups spring greens or cabbage, chopped

1 tablespoon capers

3 garlic cloves, thinly sliced

grated zest of 1 unwaxed lemon

1 tablespoon red wine vinegar

3 tablespoons fruity extra virgin olive oil (preferably Sicilian)

sea salt and freshly ground black pepper

lemon wedges and country bread, to serve

Serves 4

Put all the vegetables in a large saucepan. Add a little water (about 200 ml/¾ cup) to prevent burning and gently cook over medium heat for 8 minutes. The vegetables should all be al dente.

Drain the vegetables, add them to a serving bowl and dress with the remaining ingredients.

Garnish with lemon wedges and serve with country bread for mopping up the delicious juices.

Aubergine and pomegranate salad

Insalata di melanzane e melograno

This recipe comes from a family friend called Salvatore Veltini, in Ragusa. Ragusa is on the southern tip of the island and was a Norman stronghold that became a fief of the Cabrera dynasty. This recipe is so simple and utterly delicious. I am a stickler for salting aubergines/eggplants – it's a family thing! It also means that the aubergine/eggplant will fry better, absorb less oil and have a superior flavour.

2 medium aubergines/eggplants, cut lengthways into 4-mm/⅛-inch thick slices

3 tablespoons olive oil

grated zest and freshly squeezed juice of 2 unwaxed lemons

2 garlic cloves, finely chopped

1½ tablespoons white wine vinegar

1½ tablespoons good-quality extra virgin olive oil

a handful of mint, roughly chopped

a handful of flat-leaf parsley, roughly chopped

1 pomegranate, seeded

100 g/3½ oz. pecorino (soft or firm)

sea salt and freshly ground black pepper

Serves 4

Sprinkle the aubergine/eggplant slices with salt. Weigh down and leave for 15 minutes. Remove and pat dry with paper towels.

Heat the olive oil in a large, heavy frying pan/skillet and fry the aubergine/eggplant slices. Choose a ridged pan if you can, as the aubergine/eggplant looks far more attractive this way.

Mix the lemon zest and juice, garlic, vinegar and good oil, then mix this dressing with the aubergine/eggplant, and scatter with the chopped herbs, pomegranate seeds and pecorino. If using soft pecorino place it in dollops, if firm scatter shavings.

Black fig, mozzarella and basil salad

Insalata di fichi con mozzarella e basilico

At the height of the fig season in September, Sicily is alive with fig recipes, each region adding their own subtleties. This was enjoyed by my father and me on a lazy balmy Sunday lunch under the pergola of family friends in Siracusa. Please be sure that every ingredient is 'just so' to preserve the deliciousness of this simple salad. I dedicate this recipe to a dear friend and fig lover, Caroline Reid.

8 black or green figs, stalks trimmed and peeled

2 buffalo mozzarella balls, torn apart

a generous handful of basil, ripped

1 small shallot, finely chopped

1–2 tablespoons red wine vinegar

4 tablespoons good-quality extra virgin olive oil

sea salt and freshly ground black pepper

crusty bread, to serve

Serves 4

Halve the figs and combine with the mozzarella and basil. Scatter over the shallot, sea salt and black pepper

Mix the vinegar and olive oil together to form an emulsion and drizzle over the salad.

Serve with delicious crusty bread to mop up the juices.

Pickled cauliflower salad

Insalata di cavolfiori

1 medium cauliflower

55 g/½ cup green olives, halved and stoned/pitted

1 tablespoon good-quality capers

2 tablespoons sundried tomatoes, chopped

1 roasted red (bell) pepper, chopped into fork-friendly pieces

a handful of flat-leaf parsley, finely chopped

2 tablespoons fresh and fruity olive oil (preferably Sicilian)

2 tablespoons red wine vinegar

sea salt and freshly ground black pepper

Serves 4

Cauliflowers are at their best in the winter in Italy. Olives, too, will have just been harvested and will be used for the first time at the Christmas table. As a diehard cauliflower fan, I am so thrilled with the renaissance that cauliflower is experiencing. One great tip I've learned is that adding fresh bay leaves while cooking cauliflower dissipates the smell. In fact it works for all the brassica vegetables, including cabbage, broccoli and Brussels sprouts. The Italian name for this salad means 'reinforced salad' because it is often served at Christmas time to 'back up' or 'reinforce' the other dishes on the table, acting as a refreshing interlude between courses.

Cut the cauliflower into small, uniform-sized florets. Rinse well in cold water and drain. Put the florets in a large saucepan and add cold water to cover. Add 1 teaspoon of salt and bring to the boil. Boil for 3 minutes, then drain and refresh in cold water.

Meanwhile, in a salad bowl, combine the olives, capers, sundried tomatoes, roasted red (bell) pepper, parsley and seasoning, then mix in the cauliflower.

In a small bowl, whisk together the oil and vinegar. Add to the vegetables and mix well. Cover and marinate for 1 hour before serving.

Pantelleria potato salad

Insalata di patata di pantelleria

6 new potatoes, peeled

1 tablespoon capers, rinsed if they are salted

8 small ripe tomatoes, cut in half

8 black olives

1 small red onion, cut into thin semicircles

a sprinkle of dried oregano

3 tablespoons extra virgin olive oil

1 tablespoon red wine vinegar

sea salt and freshly ground black pepper

Serves 4

I had read about the Sicilian love of potatoes and I also knew a little from my father's business as a fruit and vegetable importer. He maintained that the rich volcanic soil was the reason that the island produces such excellent potatoes. On a visit I was amazed to see so many varieties piled high on carts along the roadside, and by the quantities that people bought. When I questioned the stallholder, he smiled and said potatoes are so versatile. And they most certainly are.

Boil the potatoes until tender – the time this takes depends on the variety and size. Drain and cool. Cut in half if large.

Arrange the potatoes on an attractive platter and mix in the remaining ingredients. Season and dress with oil and vinegar.

Braised cannellini beans with prosciutto and herbs

Fagioli con le cotiche di prosciutto

250 g/9 oz. dried cannellini beans, soaked overnight with bay leaves and a whole garlic clove

2 rosemary sprigs

2 garlic cloves, finely minced

2 tablespoons olive oil

1 onion, finely chopped

150 g/5½ oz. prosciutto, diced (buy from your deli counter)

6 ripe plum tomatoes, peeled, deseeded and roughly chopped

a handful of basil, freshly chopped

a handful of flat-leaf parsley, freshly chopped

1 tablespoon extra virgin olive oil

sea salt and freshly ground black pepper

Serves 4–6

This deliciously rustic, hearty salad is just a perfect dish for sharing at family gatherings.

Discard the bean soaking water and replace with fresh water in a large saucepan. Place the rosemary and garlic in the pan and bring to the boil. After 10 minutes reduce the heat and cook for a further 1 hour 20 minutes until tender. Drain and set aside.

Heat the olive oil in a medium-sized frying pan/skillet and fry the onion until golden. Add the prosciutto and fry until it is golden too.

Stir in the tomatoes, basil and parsley. Season with salt and pepper. Add the cannellini beans, adjust the seasoning and stir in the extra virgin olive oil to serve.

Baked tomatoes filled with rice and Parmesan

Pomodori ripieni all forno con riso e parmigiano

Sicilian tomatoes are undoubtedly the best, thriving in the abundant light, great fertile soil and dry conditions. It was on a business trip with my father many years ago that I was introduced to a variety in Siracusa called Pachino. He imported this variety from Sicily and they became so very popular. This recipe was produced at a memorable lunch in honour of my father's visit and to celebrate the tomato that the producer was so proud of. Because the ingredients are all so simple, please ensure that they are of the very best quality. Great olive oil is essential as it will breathe life into every dish you make. Never compromise.

8 medium ripe tomatoes

4 small old potatoes, peeled

100 g/¾ cup cooked Arborio risotto rice

2 garlic cloves, finely chopped

100 g/1½ cups Parmesan cheese, freshly grated

3 generous handfuls of fresh flat-leaf parsley

2 generous handfuls of fresh basil, chopped or torn

a handful of mint, freshly chopped, plus extra leaves to garnish

½ teaspoon dried oregano

2 tablespoons olive oil

sea salt and freshly ground black pepper

2 tablespoons extra virgin olive oil

Serves 4–6

Make a horizontal slit across the stem end of the tomatoes, as if cutting off a small slice, but do not cut all the way through – this creates a hinged lid. Using a teaspoon, carefully hollow out the tomatoes and finely chop the extracted pulp. Transfer the pulp to a bowl and set aside. Salt the inside of the tomatoes and place them upside down, hinge open, to drain.

Cut the potatoes into matchsticks, approx. 10 cm/4 inches long and 2.5 cm/1 inch wide. Salt the potatoes and set aside.

Preheat the oven to 180°C (350°F) Gas 4. Oil a baking dish.

Place the rice, garlic, cheese, parsley, basil, mint, oregano and olive oil in a bowl, add the reserved tomato pulp, mix well and season with salt and pepper. Stuff the tomatoes, leaving 2 cm/¾ inch at the top and press down on the lid. Arrange the stuffed tomatoes in the baking dish. Place the potato matchsticks standing up between the tomatoes.

Bake for 30 minutes in the preheated oven. Remove from the oven and serve hot or warm, garnished with mint and drizzled with extra virgin olive oil.

The Sicilian citrus groves

Lemons and oranges are often the first things that pop into people's heads when they think of Sicily. The unspoiled sunshine and rich soil create unique citrus fruits that are famous around the world.

FAR LEFT After an abundant lemon harvest,the fruits are carefully sorted and packed into sturdy wicker baskets.

TOP LEFT In a Sicilian citrus grove, the sun-ripened oranges are ready for picking.

CENTRE LEFT The rich, jewel colours of oranges, pomegranates and grapefruit create an eye-catching display on a market stall.

BOTTOM LEFT Bottles of the Italian liqueur limoncello, made from the zest of lemons.

Citrus fruits were originally indigenous to the Far East, and were brought westwards to the Middle East, then to North Africa and the wider Mediterranean region by Arab conquerors in the 9th and 10th centuries.

Lemons and bitter oranges are known to have arrived in Sicily around 830 AD. Gardens of these citrus trees were planted all around Sicily by skilled gardeners who the Arabs brought with them. These gardeners built remarkable networks of underground tunnels, known as *qanats*, to store rainwater so that the trees could be irrigated during the summer months. These ingenious qanats still exist, all around the major urban centres of Sicily, including the capital, Palermo. In Palermo, it is still possible (although not especially comfortable) to access these tunnels and travel from one side of the city to another. This is one of the reasons that the Mafia were so keen to get control of the citrus farms here in the 1980s, as they came complete with their own underground escape systems. The Mafia were also rather keen on the EU subsidies, but that's another story.

The Palermo area used to be called the Conca d'Oro (the Golden Shell). The romantics among us think that this is because the citrus fruits glitter in the sun, but it may have something more to do with the wealth that these fruits brought to the island. Northern European naval vessels and merchant ships would buy the fruits from the Sicilian landowners in Palermo – a vital pitstop to help protect their crews from scurvy.

In May, the air in Sicily is thick with the heady perfume of lemon blossom. Sicilians are fiercely proud of their lemon trees, and rightly so! Their quality is unmatched (although some Amalfi dwellers may disagree) but the sheer scale of the lemon-growing business in Sicily is astonishing – 90% of all Italian lemons are grown there. The area around Mount Etna is well-known for its lemon groves – the volcanic soil gives the lemon a sweetness and taste that is completely unique. The lemon trees there bear fruit all year round, but they're particularly good in winter because they get more rain. Correspondingly, the lack of water in the hotter summer months can make the lemons dry and hard.

I feel I should add a word about the Sicily/Amalfi lemon rivalry. Sicilian lemons are smaller but more potent than their Amalfi cousins, with a sharpness and acidity that works particularly well when contrasted with sugar. The Amalfi lemon (the best known variety being the Sfusato Amalfitano) is highly perfumed, yet is subtler in flavour than its Sicilian cousin. So they're both wonderful, but for different reasons. No prizes for guessing where my heart lies, though!

Blood oranges are actually the main orange grown in Italy. In Sicily, some varieties of blood orange (*Arancia Rossa di Sicilia*) have attained Protected Geographical Indication (PGI) status, which means that 'the entire product must be traditionally and at least partially manufactured within the specific region'. The growers must adhere to strict production regulations in order to bear the PGI label.

The blood orange possesses unique crimson-coloured flesh. Its distinctive colour is down to the antioxidant pigments (known as anthocyanins), which turn the flesh crimson as the fruit develops during low temperatures. Blood oranges have a lovely raspberry-like flavour, as well as the typical orange citrus notes you would expect. There are three principal varieties of blood orange – the *Sanguinello* (discovered in Spain in 1929), *Tarocco* (found in Italy and thought to be a mutation of the sanguinello) and the *Moro* (also arising from a mutation of the *sanguinello* and believed to have originated in the province of Siracusa in Sicily). There are at least a dozen other less well-known varieties, too.

Crab and artichoke salad

Insalata di granchi e carciofo

A salad that I first enjoyed in Marsala, western Sicily, sitting by the beach at the end of a hot day, drinking a very dry Prosecco and enjoying the crisp flavours of the salad leaves and the stunningly fresh crab. Try to use fresh crab meat: put 10–12 live blue crabs into abundant boiled and salted water, bring back to the boil, then simmer for 10 minutes. Cool and remove the meat from the shell with a nutcracker and mallet.

a bunch of rocket/arugula

1 head of radicchio (round or long)

500 g/1 lb. 2 oz. cooked crab meat

6 cherry tomatoes, halved

4 artichoke hearts in oil, quartered

a handful of flat-leaf parsley, roughly chopped

2–3 tablespoons light (not too heavy) extra virgin olive oil

grated zest and freshly squeezed juice of 2 unwaxed lemons

sea salt and freshly ground black pepper

2 chunks of country bread, chopped into cubes and toasted

Serves 4

Wash and dry the rocket/arugula well and divide between 4 plates. Core the radicchio and then add to the rocket/arugula on the plates.

Add a quarter of the crab meat to each plate. Top with a quarter of the cherry tomatoes, artichokes and parsley.

Make up a dressing with the oil, lemon juice and seasoning. Scatter over the zest of the lemon and the croutons, and drizzle with the dressing prior to serving.

Soups
and pasta
Zuppa e pasta

Cauliflower soup

Zuppi di cavolfiori

This recipe has its roots firmly anchored in Ragusa, a Baroque town of great beauty in the south of the country, and highlights the Greek influences on Sicilian cuisine. I am thrilled that cauliflower has become so popular – it's a wonderful vegetable, full of goodness and flavour.

2 tablespoons olive oil

1 onion, chopped

2 garlic cloves, finely chopped

2 ribs/sticks celery, finely chopped

3 fresh bay leaves

8 sage leaves, plus extra to garnish

1 tablespoon lemon thyme, leaves only, plus extra to garnish

6 medium old potatoes, peeled and coarsely chopped

1 kg/2¼ lbs. cauliflower, divided into small florets

500 ml/2 cups chicken stock

sea salt and freshly ground black pepper

finely grated zest of 1 unwaxed lemon

TO SERVE

sesame bread, toasted and rubbed with a peeled garlic clove

grated Pecorino cheese

Serves 4–6

In a large saucepan, heat the oil and fry the onion. When the onion is golden, add the garlic, celery and herbs, and cook for just a few minutes, stirring frequently.

Add the potatoes, cauliflower and stock to the pan. Season. Cook over medium heat for about 20 minutes, until the vegetables are tender. Allow to cool slightly, then transfer to a food processor and blend until velvety in texture. Return to the saucepan, stir in the lemon zest and check the seasoning, adding more salt and pepper if necessary. Reheat gently before serving.

Serve with slices of the toasted sesame bread, topped with Pecorino cheese and heated gently under the grill/broiler. Garnish with a scattering of sage leaves and lemon thyme.

Courgette leaf and fresh tomato soup with pastina

Foglie di zucchine con pomodoro fresche e pastina

At long last, a recipe for courgette/zucchini leaves! The flavour is slightly bitter from the leaves, but it is balanced well with the sweetness of the tomatoes, onions and basil. It's very satisfying to make, especially if the ingredients I've listed happen to be growing in your garden! This dish originates from Messina, in the north-eastern tip of the island.

500 g/1 lb. 2 oz. courgette/zucchini leaves or chicory/endive leaves

2 tablespoons olive oil

2 onions, finely chopped

2 garlic cloves, finely chopped

500 g/2¾ cups ripe tomatoes, skinned, deseeded and roughly chopped

a handful of fresh basil

125 g/2 cups pastina or little dried pasta shapes (e.g. stars, wheels)

sea salt and freshly ground black pepper

TO SERVE
2 tablespoons good-quality extra virgin olive oil

Parmesan cheese (optional)

Serves 6-8

Cook the courgette/zucchini leaves (or chicory/endive) in plenty of rolling boiling water for 20 minutes. Drain and chop the leaves.

Heat the olive oil in a large pan and cook the onions until they are golden. Add the chopped leaves, stirring well. Add the garlic, tomatoes, basil, little pasta shapes and seasoning. Stir well and add 1½ litres/6½ cups of water.

Bring to the boil and simmer for 10 minutes, until the pasta is cooked. Season again.

Serve with plenty of Parmesan cheese and good oil to anoint the soup.

Broad bean soup with lemon, mint and pasta

Zuppa di fava con lemoni, menta e pasta

This is my version of a soup that has been the mainstay of the Sicilian peasant's diet. It's a humble and utterly divine dish, aided by the beautiful oil of the island which breathes life and flavour into the soup. This recipe celebrates the island's multicultural heritage, as Greek and Spanish food all show their love of the broad/fava bean. On 13th June, these beans are eaten to celebrate the feast day of St Anthony.

400 g/3½ cups dried broad/fava beans

2 fennel bulbs, finely chopped

3 garlic cloves, chopped

grated zest and freshly squeezed juice of 1 unwaxed lemon

2 tablespoons olive oil

200 g/7 oz. dried pasta (very small shapes, such as ditalini or faro)

a very generous handful of fresh mint

4 tablespoons good-quality extra virgin olive oil

sea salt and freshly ground black pepper

good crusty bread, to serve

 Serves 4–6

Soak the broad/fava beans overnight in plenty of water.

The next day, drain the beans. Place them in a large saucepan with water 2.5 cm/1 inch above the beans (they will swell to three times their volume). Bring to the boil and simmer for at least 1 hour until thre beans open up and come apart.

Add the fennel, garlic, lemon zest and juice, olive oil and salt and pepper to taste.

Continue cooking for 25 minutes, adding the pasta 10 minutes before serving, followed by the mint. The soup should be thick but not too thick (e.g. the consistency of single/light cream). Adjust the seasoning and anoint with extra virgin olive oil. Serve with good bread.

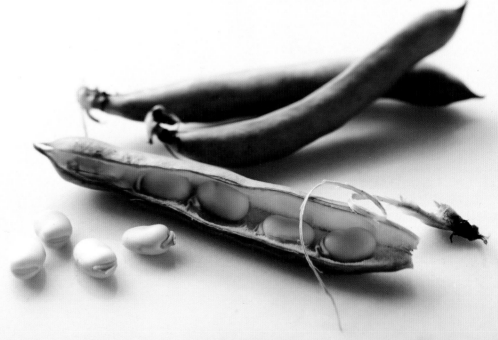

Beef broth with tiny meatballs

Polpettine in brodo di carne

1½ litres/6½ cups good beef broth
or flavoursome meat stock

100 g/1⅓ cups dried pasta
(I like ditalini – tiny pasta tubes)

MEATBALLS

250 g/9 oz. good-quality minced/
ground beef steak

75 g/1 cup finely grated Parmesan cheese,
plus extra to serve

75 g/1⅓ cups fresh breadcrumbs,
blitzed in a blender to fine crumbs

1 UK large/US extra large egg

a handful of flat-leaf parsley, finely chopped,
plus extra to garnish

grated zest of 1 unwaxed lemon

1 garlic clove, finely chopped

sea salt and freshly ground black pepper

Serves 4-6

This hearty dish harks from Adrano in the province of Catania. It's a simple soup filled with wonderful childhood memories for me. It's traditionally eaten at Easter, on Holy Thursday.

To make the meatballs, put all the ingredients in a large mixing bowl and mix with a wooden spoon to combine.

Use lightly floured hands to roll tiny meatballs, about the size of hazelnuts. Set them aside on a plate as you go and repeat until all the meatball mixture has been used.

Pour the broth into a large saucepan and bring to a simmer over medium heat. Drop in the meatballs and cook over medium heat for about 20 minutes. Add the pasta and continue to cook for a further 8–10 minutes, until the pasta is al dente and the meatballs are cooked through.

Ladle into soup plates to serve. Garnish with flat-leaf parsley and offer additional Parmesan cheese for sprinkling.

Mussels and bucatini pasta

Bucatini e cozza

350 g/12½ oz. dried bucatini or linguine

a generous handful of fresh flat-leaf parsley

3 tablespoons extra virgin olive oil

sea salt and freshly ground black pepper

MUSSEL SAUCE

10 ripe plum tomatoes

2 tablespoons olive oil

3 garlic cloves, chopped

2 teaspoons crushed dried chilli/chile (peperoncino)

40 mussels, cleaned and debearded

1 rib/stick celery, finely chopped

20 Gaeta olives, stoned/pitted

50 ml/3 tablespoons dry white wine

a handful of basil leaves, roughly torn

sea salt and freshly ground black pepper

Serves 4

A simple but memorable combination enjoyed in Siracusa when the mussels are the sweetest in flavour. Long pasta is always favoured for seafood sauces.

For the sauce, immerse the tomatoes in a bowl of boiling water for 10 seconds to loosen the skins, then drain and peel away the skins. Chop the tomato flesh.

Heat the oil in a large, heavy-based sauté pan. Add the garlic and chilli/chile and sauté until lightly golden. Add the mussels, cover the pan with a tight fitting lid and cook for 4–6 minutes until the shells have opened. Discard any mussels that remain closed.

Meanwhile, add the pasta to a large pan of rolling boiling salted water and cook until al dente.

Add the tomatoes, celery, olives and wine to the mussels and cook until the wine has evaporated, about 1 minute. Season and add the basil.

Drain the pasta and toss with the parsley and extra virgin olive oil. Combine with the mussels and eat immediately.

Spaghetti with lobster sauce

Spaghetti con salsa di aragostina

3 small live lobsters or lobster tails, weighing about 400 g/14 oz. each

3 tablespoons olive oil

2 garlic cloves, chopped

a generous pinch of crushed dried chilli/chile (peperoncino)

125 ml/½ cup dry white wine

a handful of fresh flat-leaf parsley, roughly chopped

350 g/12½ oz. dried spaghetti

sea salt and freshly ground black pepper

2 tablespoons fine Sicilian extra virgin olive oil, for drizzling

Serves 4

The best lobsters are tiny, sweet and found on Sicily's south-west coast. The richness of their flavour contrasts wonderfully with the simplicity of the spaghetti. Serve with bread for mopping up juices.

Bring a large saucepan of salted water to the boil and drop in the lobster. Simmer for 12 minutes and drain. Leave to cool.

Halve the lobsters and remove the flesh from the bodies, discarding the stomach sacks. Crack the pincers and remove the meat. Keep to one side.

Heat the olive oil in a sauté pan and add the garlic and chilli/chile. Sauté for a couple of minutes, then add the wine, lobster meat and parsley, and simmer for 4 more minutes. Season with salt and pepper.

Cook the spaghetti in plenty of rolling boiling salted water until al dente, then drain. Toss with the lobster sauce, and drizzle with a good, not-too-strong olive oil. Serve at once.

Tagliatelle with courgette flowers and chicken

Tagliatelle ai fiori di zucchine con pollo

This Trapanese-style pasta dish is colourful and tasty, and is best served in the early summer when courgette/zucchini flowers are plentiful. This dish will produce gasps of approval from family and friends.

2 skinless chicken breasts, preferably organic, 350 g/12½ oz. in total

50 g/3 tablespoons unsalted butter

2 tablespoons olive oil

1 small onion, thinly sliced

200 g/2 cups small courgettes/zucchini, thickness of a finger, cut into thin julienne strips

1 garlic clove, crushed

2 teaspoons finely chopped fresh marjoram

350 g/12½ oz. dried tagliatelle

a large handful of courgette/zucchini flowers, thoroughly washed and stamens removed

sea salt and freshly ground black pepper

thinly shaved Parmesan cheese, to garnish

Serves 4-6

Heat the grill/broiler to medium. Season the chicken and grill/broil for 25 minutes, turning once, until golden and cooked through. Cut into evenly sized pieces and put to one side.

Heat the butter and half the olive oil in a medium saucepan, add the onion and cook gently, stirring frequently, for about 5 minutes until softened. Add the courgettes/zucchini to the pan and sprinkle over the garlic, marjoram and salt and pepper to taste.

Add the chicken pieces and cook for 8 minutes until the courgettes/zucchini have coloured.

Set aside a few whole courgette/zucchini flowers to garnish, then roughly shred the rest and add them to the pan. Stir to mix, taste and adjust the seasoning if required.

Meanwhile, cook the pasta in rolling boiling salted water until al dente. Drain the cooked pasta and tip it into the chicken mixture with the remaining oil. Serve with Parmesan cheese shavings and the reserved courgette/zucchini flowers.

Rigatoni alla Norma with ricotta

Rigatoni alla Norma con ricotta

This recipe hails from the province of Catania, on the east coast of Sicily. It is named after the opera 'Norma', by Vincenzo Bellini. This dish is made even more special by using super-ripe plum tomatoes.

1 kg/2¼ lbs. fresh ripe plum tomatoes, for colour and flavour

3 tablespoons olive oil

1 onion, finely chopped

2 garlic cloves, finely chopped

1 tablespoon tomato purée/paste

1 large aubergine/eggplant

350 g/12½ oz. dried rigatoni

sea salt and freshly ground black pepper

3–4 tablespoons freshly grated ricotta salata, or young pecorino or Parmesan or even mozzarella (ricotta salata is traditional – it is a dry, slightly salty ricotta)

a generous handful of fresh basil

2 tablespoons fruity Sicilian extra virgin olive oil, to serve

Serves 4

Plunge the tomatoes into boiling water for 30 seconds to loosen the skins, then peel and quarter them. Heat 1 tablespoon of olive oil in a large saucepan, add the onion and when coloured, add the garlic, tomatoes and tomato purée/paste. Season with salt and pepper and cook gently for 15 minutes.

Cut the aubergine/eggplant into 2-cm/¾-inch cubes and place in a bowl. Sprinkle with salt, weigh down and leave for 15 minutes. Rinse the salt off, pat dry and fry in the remaining olive oil until golden.

Cook the rigatoni in rolling boiling salted water until al dente. Drain and add to the tomato mixture, followed by the aubergine/eggplant mixture and re-season.

Serve with the ricotta salata, basil and extra virgin olive oil.

Pasta with sardines

Pasta con le sardine

350 g/12½ oz. dried spaghetti

fennel fronds, to garnish

2 tablespoons extra virgin olive oil, not too strong

PANGRATTATO

1 garlic clove, finely chopped

1 tablespoon olive oil

150 g/5¼ oz. open-textured, crustless sourdough-type bread, blitzed into breadcumbs

sea salt and freshly ground black pepper

SAUCE

1 tablespoon olive oil

50 g/¾ cup pine nuts

1 garlic clove, finely chopped

1 large fennel bulb (reserve the fronds), finely sliced

1 onion, chopped

100 ml/7 tablespoons dry white wine

6 butterflied sardines, pin boned

6 anchovies in oil

50 g/⅓ cup (dark) raisins

Serves 4

This is the classic Sicilian pasta dish. The version that I most enjoyed, and I really have tried so, so many variations, includes wild fennel and anchovies. I hope you enjoy my favourite dish!

Preheat the oven to 180°C (350°F) Gas 4.

To make the pangrattato (breadcrumbs), combine the garlic, olive oil, bread, and salt and pepper to taste on a parchment-lined baking sheet. Bake for approximately 6 minutes, stirring occasionally, until golden. Cool and blend or process until fine, either in a pestle and mortar or food processor.

To make the sauce, heat the olive oil in a large frying pan/skillet, add the pine nuts and stir until golden. Add the finely chopped garlic, fennel and onion and cook until tender. Add the wine, sardines, anchovies and raisins and simmer for 8 minutes on low heat. There will be an amazing aroma by now.

Cook the spaghetti in rolling boiling salted water and drain, reserving a little of the water to slacken the sardine sauce.

Mix the pasta and sardines together, and scatter generously with the breadcrumbs and fennel fronds. Drizzle with the olive oil and serve immediately.

Pappardelle with duck ragù

Pappardelle con anatra

It doesn't get much better than this – a rich, full-flavoured ragù of duck braised with white wine, pancetta and fresh bay and rosemary, tossed with ribbons of homemade fresh pasta. Serve this delicious treat with a simple salad of bitter radiccho leaves.

DUCK SAUCE

2 tablespoons olive oil

2 onions, finely chopped

100 g/3½ oz. pancetta, cubed

3 bay leaves (fresh are best)

3 garlic cloves, crushed

250 ml/1 cup dry white wine

3 sprigs rosemary

1 tablespoon tomato purée/paste

1 kg/2¼ lbs. duck, skin-on

250 ml/1 cup chicken stock

grated Parmesan cheese, to serve

a handful of flat-leaf parsley, freshly chopped, to serve

PAPPARDELLE

300 g/2 cups plus 2 tablespoons Italian '00' flour

300 g/1¾ cups semolina, plus extra for rolling

3 UK large/US extra large eggs

a splash of olive oil

Serves 6

Preheat the oven to 150°C (300°F) Gas 2.

To make the duck ragù, heat the oil in a casserole dish over medium heat and add the onions, pancetta and bay leaves. When coloured, add the garlic, stirring occasionally, then add the wine, rosemary and tomato purée/paste. Keep warm.

Meanwhile, cook the duck, skin-side down, in a large sauté pan. Cook until the skin turns golden, then transfer to the casserole dish, adding the chicken stock. Cover the casserole with a lid and cook for at least 2½ hours in the preheated oven until the meat falls off the bone.

Remove the duck from the casserole, strip the meat (not the skin), and put it back in the casserole with the juices. Adjust the seasoning and continue cooking for at least 30 minutes.

To make the pappardelle, combine the flour and semolina together on a work surface. Make a hole in the middle and crack in the eggs, one at a time, followed by the oil. Mix the eggs with a fork until broken from their yolks. When the mixture falls from the fork in a fine stream, start flicking in the flours until the mixture resembles a paste. Massage the pasta until it becomes strong and soft like silk; this should take approximately 7 minutes. The mixture should be as smooth as marble and springy to the touch. Roll flat and leave to rest in the fridge for 15–20 minutes, covered in clingfilm/plastic wrap.

Divide the pasta into 3 equal pieces. Roll each piece through a pasta machine, notch by notch. Do not take it to the last notch as that would make it too thin. Sprinkle the pasta with semolina if it is sticking. When you have three long strips, leave them dry. The time this takes will very much depend on the temperature around you; you want it to be not too dry and not too damp.

Cut the pieces of pasta by hand into 2.5 cm/1 inch wide strips.

To cook, place the pasta in a generous pan of rolling boiling salted water. Cook for 5 minutes; the pasta will obediently rise to the top of the pan. Strain and stir into the warm duck sauce. Serve with Parmesan cheese, chopped parsley and a simple radiccho salad if liked. Eat straight away.

Potato gnocchi with chicken sauce

Gnocchi di patate con sabre di pollo

Light and fluffy like clouds – that is what gnocchi should be. They are so easy to make and enjoyed all over Italy, especially Sicily. I claim that gnocchi is the whole reason why I am married (my husband loves them). It's served with a really good chicken sauce that I first enjoyed in the Caltanissetta province in central Sicily. This area is the heart of Sicily's 'Wild West', featuring dramatic and harsh, yet enticing landscapes.

POTATO GNOCCHI

750 g/1 lb. 10 oz. even-sized floury old potatoes

150 g/1 cup plus 3 tablespoons Italian '00' flour

1 teaspoon sea salt

1 UK large/US extra large egg, lightly beaten

1 tablespoon olive oil

CHICKEN SAUCE

2 tablespoons olive oil

1 onion, chopped

50 g/½ cup unsmoked pancetta, cubed

4 skin-on large boneless chicken thighs (preferably organic), cut into fork-friendly chunks

100 g/¾ cup stoned/pitted green olives

3 fresh bay leaves

1 garlic clove, crushed

2 tablespoons tomato purée/paste (or estratto, see page 77)

125 ml/½ cup dry white wine

50 g/2 cups dried porcini mushrooms (soaked for 10 minutes in cold water; reserve the soaking water for the dish)

100 g/1½ cups chestnut mushrooms

1 tablespoon fresh rosemary, finely chopped

150 ml/⅔ cup chicken stock

sea salt and freshly ground black pepper

a handful of flat-leaf parsley, chopped

Parmesan cheese, to serve

Serves 6-8

Preheat the oven to 200°C (400°F) Gas 6.

Place the potatoes on a baking sheet lined with parchment and bake in the preheated oven for 40–45 minutes. When the potatoes are tender, they are cooked. Leave to cool slightly.

Meanwhile, to make the chicken sauce, heat the olive oil in a casserole dish set over medium heat, add the onion and cook until golden. Add the pancetta and cook for about 6 minutes.

Add the chicken and stir fry for 10 minutes, then add the rest of the ingredients, except the parsley and Parmesan cheese. Simmer, covered, for 30 minutes. Stir occasionally, adding a little of the reserved mushroom soaking water if the mixture is becoming dry.

When the potatoes have cooled, cut them in half and scoop out the flesh. Place the flesh in a ricer or mouli grater and process directly onto the work surface. Scatter the flour around the riced potatoes, make a well in the centre and add the salt and the egg. Mix gently until a soft dough forms. Add more flour as needed, taking care not to overwork the dough. Shape it into long, narrow logs. Wrap each log in clingfilm/plastic wrap and leave to rest in the fridge for 10 minutes.

Roll the dough into narrow sausages, 1 cm/½ inch thick, then cut into short 2-cm/¾-inch pieces and pinch the gnocchi to create texture for the sauce. You may like to roll the gnocchi over the back of the tines of a fork. Set aside on a floured tray and keep covered.

Bring a large pan of salted water to a rolling boil and drop in the gnocchi in batches. When the gnocchi rise to the surface, count to 30, then remove the gnocchi and drain.

Taste the chicken sauce, adjust the seasoning if necessary and add the parsley. The sauce should be flavoursome and a good consistency, not too thick. If it is, add some water.

Pour the hot chicken sauce over the cooked gnocchi and serve with Parmesan cheese, if desired.

Tomato sauce with almonds

Salse di pomodori con mandorla

1 kg/2¼ lbs. ripe plum tomatoes, peeled and chopped

2 garlic cloves, finely chopped

a generous handful of basil, freshly chopped

a generous handful of flat-leaf parsley, freshly chopped

75 g/¾ cup blanched almonds, finely chopped

a small pinch of crushed dried chilli/chile (peperoncino)

2 tablespoons olive oil

350 g/9 oz. dried spaghetti or tagliatelle

sea salt and freshly ground black pepper

freshly grated caciocavallo cheese (or if you can't find it, provolone cheese), to serve

2 tablespoons good-quality extra virgin olive oil, for drizzling

Serves 4

I believe this tasty, satisfying and easy-to-make pesto originates from the Trapani province, but it is available in all good trattorias throughout the island, often listed on the menu as pasta picchi pacchi. Sicily really does grow the finest tomatoes, said to be connected to the light and the fertile soil.

Mix the tomatoes, garlic, basil, parsley, almonds, chilli/chile and salt and pepper in a bowl with olive oil. Leave to marinate for at least 2 hours. Adjust the seasoning if required.

Cook the pasta in a large pan of rolling boiling salted water. Drain, and mix the tomato sauce with the pasta.

Serve with the caciocavallo cheese and drizzle with the olive oil. Serve straight away.

Tomato paste extract

Pasta di pomodori estratto

'Strattu (the dialect word for *estratto*) is a thick tomato paste that Sicilians make along with their annual supply of tomato sauce and it livens up pasta sauces no end. No Sicilian would make a pork ragù without adding a goodly dollop of 'strattu and I find a little of it adds depth to any recipe requiring tomato sauce.

Made with only ripe Italian plum tomatoes, salt and oil, estratto is evident in every village in Sicily and is made with pride — pride in the beautiful tomatoes and pride in nature, as the sun 'cooks' the tomatoes into a strong, pungent, delicious extract. This extract can be enjoyed through the year, added to sauces, casseroles, soups and even spread on toasted bread. Cooked tomatoes are forced through a food mill and strained. The tomato residue is then spread onto a large wooden board and left in the sun to dry. After a couple of hours the mixture is stirred with a little salt as this helps to concentrate the mixture, which reduces to a tenth of its original volume. This process takes about 4 days and it is nature that really does the work, as the sun concentrates the tomatoes. When bottled, a layer of oil covers the tomatoes and acts as a preservative.

Pistachio pesto

Pesto di pistacchi

Sicily is the only place in Italy where pistachios are grown. The city of Bronte is perched at the top of volcanic rock, located about half a mile north east of Etna. The Arabs, who once controlled the region, are responsible for bringing pistachio trees to Sicily from the Middle East. The Sicilian word for pistachio is 'frastuca', derived from the Arab 'fustuq', which refers to a forest of pistachio trees. The 'Bronte' variety of pistachio are eaten daily by old and young alike. The market places in Sicily are covered with their shells.

On a recent trip to Sicily I saw a group of young men entering a darkened shop – the only indication that it was a shop was the sack placed outside the door – I followed, and was thrilled to find every imaginable nut, seed and pulse displayed in vast colourful mountains in the cool, cavernous space. Needless to say I was in paradise! In the corner, a group of old men 'pas a tempo' (passing the time of day) eagerly coaxed me to try before I buy. We became firm friends and I returned daily to stock up, particularly on pistachios. What impressed me were the young people eating nuts from the cones of paper that were so dextrously put together by Claudio, the owner.

Inspired by my experience, I put together a recipe for pistachio pesto. It's wonderful on pasta, bruschetta, risotto and much more. It also makes a super gift.

200 g/7 oz. shelled unsalted pistachio nuts

1 garlic clove

50 g/¾ cup pecorino cheese, grated

50 g/¾ cup Parmesan cheese, grated

a handful of fresh basil

a handful of fresh flat-leaf parsley

4 tablespoons olive oil

sea salt and freshly ground black pepper

Serves 4

Place all the ingredients in a food processor and blend until smooth, or how you like it. I love my pesto to be slightly chunky. Serve enrobed over freshly cooked pasta with extra Parmesan on top. Enjoy.

The wines of Sicily

Sicily's soil is extremely fertile, due to the nutrient-rich black ash deposited by its volcano, Mount Etna, during its eruptions. As a result, agriculture flourishes on the island, helped considerably by the warm, dry climate. As with the rest of southern Italy, the principal products are wheat, oranges, lemons, tomatoes, olives, figs, pistachios and artichokes. Two other distinctive products are citrons (a very Italian member of the citrus family), and grape vines, used to make Sicilian wines.

FAR LEFT Neatly regimented rows of Marsala grape vines, in the Trapani region of Sicily. The concrete supports between the vines are strung with wires, to support the vines as they grow.

CENTRE LEFT A beautifully detailed botanical drawing of a grape vine and its fruit.

TOP LEFT A pedestrianised walkway in the beautiful old city of Marsala.

LEFT Wooden wine barrels nestle on a specially made curved stone plinth, overlooking the vineyards.

BOTTOM LEFT The snow-covered slopes of Mount Etna dominate the skyline. Situated in the east of the island, Mount Etna is one of the world's most active volcanoes.

Sicily is now the third largest wine-producing region in Italy (itself the largest wine-producing country in the world). Grape vines were brought to the island by the Greeks, when Sicily was part of Magna Graecia (around 750 BC). In Homer's *Odyssey*, Odysseus is captured by Polyphemus, one of the Cyclopes, on an island generally thought to have been Sicily. Odysseus gets him drunk on local wine, then, by blinding him with a stake through his solitary eye, manages to make his escape. The Ancient Romans also were familiar with many early Sicilian wines.

The most familiar Sicilian wine must be Marsala, produced in and around the ancient city of the same name on the eastern tip of the island. A version of this wine had been enjoyed by locals for centuries, but it is said that when the British military were based in the city in the early 1800s, they saw its potential, thinking that Marsala wine had many of the same characteristics as sherry, port and Madeira, which were hugely popular in Britain. So, like port, the wine was fortified with brandy during its fermentation to help it survive the long journey from the Mediterranean. Later, Admiral Horatio Nelson was said to be a fan.

Marsala is produced from many different grapes, but mainly Grillo. It comes in three different types: *ambra* (amber in colour), *oro* (gold) and *rubino* (ruby red). The first two are made with white grapes, the third with red. Marsala is also classified according to age and sweetness. The minimum ageing time is one year, but a Marsala Superiore Riserva must have been aged for at least four years in oak, and up to six years. The wines must have a minimum alcohol content of 17 per cent. Early wines had brandy or a cooked must added; many modern Marsalas do not have any additions.

Marsala may have had a chequered history since the 1800s, but after a few years of neglect, producers on Sicily have made many improvements, and it has become popular again. It used to be drunk between the first and second courses of a meal, or served with a good cheese or dessert. Now it is served as an aperitif or after-dinner drink. It is also useful in cooking, making a wonderful sauce for chicken or veal, and is used in the desserts *zabaglione* and *tiramisu*.

Dessert wines, known as *passito* wines, are also found in Sicily. These are made from dried and semi-dried grapes, and are perfect with Sicilian pastries. The two best known come from small islands (also volcanic) not far from Sicily – the Malvasia of Lipari and the Moscato of Pantelleria (where some of the best capers in the world are found). Muscat grapes were brought in by the Arabs, around the 10th century AD, and dried, principally for the production of raisins.

Sicily was known in the past as the '*isola del vino*' (the island of wine), but many wines were made from bland white grapes. Since the 1980s, however, Sicily has been undergoing a wine revolution, with enthusiastic new wine-makers introducing new grape varieties and techniques. The Grillo grape, used to make the best Marsala, produces dry, crisp white wines, and Carricante (a grape grown on the slopes of Etna) has the tang of citrus – one of the island's most predominant flavours. Perhaps the best Sicilian wine, however, is a red wine made from the Nero d'Avola grape. This originates from Sicily (named for a small town near Siracusa) and is used in a number of other delicious reds, such as Cerasuolo di Vittoria. Many high-quality wines are also produced using non-native grapes, such as Syrah, Merlot and Chardonnay. The wines of Sicily, whether red, white or fortified, are well worth exploring.

Frittata lasagne

Frittata lasagne

Ideal for gluten-intolerant guests, but don't reserve this dish just for them. It is so, so good. You can be imaginative with your fillings. I just love spinach, and the colour of this dish reminds me of the Italian flag.

8 UK large/US extra large eggs

125 g/2 cups Parmesan cheese, grated, plus extra for the top of the dish

a handful of basil, finely chopped

a handful of flat-leaf parsley, finely chopped

4 tablespoons olive oil

125 g/4½ oz. passata/strained tomatoes or good homemade tomato sauce

200 g/9 oz. ricotta salata (pressed, salted, dried and aged ricotta) or buffalo mozzarella, grated

250 g/4½ cups spinach, chopped and stems removed

sea salt and freshly ground black pepper

Serves 4

Combine the eggs and Parmesan cheese in a bowl, season with salt and pepper and add the basil and parsley.

Heat 1 tablespoon of the oil in a large frying pan/skillet and add 3 tablespoons of the egg mixture. Cook over medium heat for 4 minutes to make a frittata. Flip the frittata and cook the other side until lightly golden on both sides. Remove from the pan and continue until all the oil and egg mixture is used up and you have a stack of frittatas.

Preheat the oven to 200°C (400°F) Gas 6. Grease an ovenproof dish and cut the frittatas into strips.

Place a layer of passata/strained tomatoes in the dish, then frittata strips, then ricotta or mozzarella and a handful of spinach. Continue in this way, until you have three layers.

Scatter over a thin layer of Parmesan cheese to cover the top. Cover with foil and bake in the preheated oven for about 20 minutes, until bubbling. Serve hot.

Meat
and fish

Carne e pesce

Braised lemon chicken

Pollo al limone

A light lemony chicken casserole from Ragusa, this just needs a little mountain bread (see page 114) to mop up the juices and perhaps a leafy salad to follow.

8 chicken thighs (preferably organic), bone in and skin on

2–3 tablespoons Italian '00' flour

3 tablespoons olive oil

thinly pared zest of 3 unwaxed lemons

1 small onion, chopped

2 sage sprigs

240 ml/1 cup dry white wine

60 ml/¼ cup water

sea salt and freshly ground black pepper

Serves 4

Pat the chicken pieces dry with paper towels, then dust them lightly with flour all over.

Heat the olive oil in a large, heavy sauté pan over medium-high heat. Add the chicken pieces to the pan and brown well on all sides. Using a slotted spoon, transfer the chicken to a plate and season with salt and pepper.

Reduce the heat to medium-low and add the lemon zest, onion and sage to the oil remaining in the pan. Sauté until the onion is golden and tender, about 10 minutes.

Return the chicken to the pan, along with the juices that have accumulated on the plate. Pour the wine over the chicken, partially cover the pan and simmer gently for 50–55 minutes, or until the chicken is very tender and most of the wine has evaporated. The chicken should be nutty brown in colour and glazed with the pan juices. Check the seasoning.

Arrange the chicken pieces on warm plates. Skim the fat from the pan juices, then taste and adjust the seasoning. If too thick, stir in 1–2 tablespoons water. Pour the juices over the chicken and serve.

Chicken with salmoriglio

Pollo alla salmoriglio

This salmoriglio sauce typifies Sicilian cuisine. It is wonderful with lamb, seafood and swordfish (and even steak, according to my husband). It is easy to make and have ready in the fridge. I grow a good deal of oregano especially for this dish.

1 chicken (preferably organic), 1.8 kg/4 lbs., butterflied

1 tablespoon olive oil

1 tablespoon fresh rosemary

2 garlic cloves, finely chopped

SALMORIGLIO

1 garlic clove, crushed

2 bunches of oregano (or 1 good handful)

60 ml/4 tablespoons extra virgin olive oil

freshly squeezed juice of 1 lemon

sea salt and freshly ground black pepper

2 lemons, cut into wedges, to serve

Serves 4–6

Place the chicken in a sealable plastic bag with the oil, rosemary and garlic. Season well, seal the bag and massage the chicken through the bag to coat well. Marinate in the fridge for at least 2 hours. Bring the chicken back to room temperature before cooking. Transfer the chicken to a casserole dish.

Preheat the oven to 180°C (350°F) Gas 4.

Roast the chicken in the preheated oven until browned and the juices run clear when the thigh is pierced with a skewer, approximately 35–40 minutes.

For the salmoriglio, pound the garlic with a generous pinch of salt to a paste, add the oregano and chop to a paste, then add to a jug/pitcher with the oil, lemon juice and black pepper. Serve with the chicken with lemon wedges for squeezing over.

Pan-fried spring lamb with herbs and anchovy sauce

Abbacchio alla cacciatovia

This is a dish my family and I enjoyed in the Donnafugata winery, in Marsala.

4 tablespoons olive oil

750 g/1 lb. 10 oz. new spring lamb, cut into rough chunks

2 garlic cloves, chopped

2 tablespoons freshly chopped rosemary

1 tablespoon freshly chopped sage

1 tablespoon Italian '00' flour

3 tablespoons red wine vinegar

225 ml/1 cup water

4 salt-packed anchovies, filleted

sea salt and freshly ground black pepper

4 sprigs of fresh rosemary, to garnish

Serves 4

Heat the oil in a large frying pan/skillet over medium heat, add the lamb and cook until seared on all sides. Season with salt and pepper.

Add the garlic, rosemary and sage, and dust with flour. Mix well and when the flavours have thoroughly blended, approximately 3 minutes, reduce the heat to low, add the vinegar and water and cook for 15 minutes, stirring occasionally. Add more vinegar and water if needed to prevent sticking.

Meanwhile, heat 1–2 tablespoons of the cooking liquid from the lamb in a small frying pan/skillet over medium heat. Chop the anchovies and add them to the pan/skillet, stirring until they disintegrate, approximately 3 minutes.

Pour the anchovy sauce over the lamb and cook for 4 minutes, stirring to coat the lamb. Cover and cook for 4–6 minutes. Check that the meat is tender and serve garnished with rosemary.

Falsomagro beef and pork

Falsomagro involtini

Falsomagro translates as 'fake lean'. No one can tell me the exact meaning – perhaps it's because there is a lot of stuffing and only a little meat in the portions served?

2 eggs

150 g/5½ oz. lean minced/ground pork

2 Sicilian-style sausages or other good-quality pork sausages (remove casing)

extra virgin olive oil

1 onion, sliced

800 g/1 lb. 12 oz. very thinly sliced sirloin beef

3 slices bacon

50 g/¾ cup pecorino cheese, grated

1 garlic clove, finely chopped

125 ml/½ cup red wine

vegetable or chicken stock, as required (approx. 500 ml/2 cups in total)

sea salt and freshly ground black pepper

Serves 4–6

Boil the eggs for 6 minutes, then shell them, slice them and set aside.

Prepare the stuffing for the roast by mixing the minced/ground pork with the skinned sausages. Sauté for 10 minutes in a small quantity of oil, adding half the onion.

Lay out the slices of beef on the work surface, in a rectangle and overlapping them slightly. Spread with the sautéed pork and sausage meat mixture. Add the slices of bacon, the sliced hard-boiled eggs, pecorino cheese and garlic, then season with salt and pepper. Roll up into a long sausage shape and tie with kitchen string/twine in several places along the length, to prevent it unwrapping.

Put some oil and the rest of the sliced onion in a casserole dish over medium heat. Add the stuffed roast and brown all over. Pour over the red wine and let it evaporate, then lower the heat and continue to cook uncovered for 1 hour, adding stock a little at a time.

Serve in thick slices, with the onions and sauce.

Grilled herb-stuffed pork skewers with bay leaves

Involtini di maiale al forno

This recipe hails from the San Domenico Palace Hotel in Taormina – the chef, Massimo Mantarro, was persuaded to jot down the bones of this recipe. I think you'll agree that it's simple and very tasty.

100 g/3½ oz. pancetta, smoked or unsmoked, diced

1 garlic clove, crushed

1 UK large/US extra large egg

2 tablespoons chopped fresh flat-leaf parsley

1 thick slice of country-style bread, soaked in warm water for 10 minutes and squeezed dry

750 g/1 lb. 10 oz pork loin, cut into 12 thin slices

6 x 5-cm/2-inch squares of country bread

approximately 36 fresh bay leaves

100 ml/7 tablespoons olive oil

sea salt and freshly ground black pepper

6 skewers

Serves 4-6

Put the pancetta, garlic, egg, parsley, bread and salt in a bowl and mix well.

Gently beat the pork slices until uniformly thin. Spread each slice with a dollop of the pancetta mixture. Roll into cylinders and tie with kitchen string/twine.

Preheat a grill/broiler or barbecue/outdoor grill and coat the grill rack with oil. Thread each of the skewers with 2 pork bundles separated by bread squares and fresh bay leaves. Arrange the skewers on a baking sheet, drizzle with oil and season well with salt and pepper. Grill/broil over medium heat for 10–15 minutes, turning so that all sides are cooked evenly. Serve at once.

Veal with artichokes and broad beans

Vitello con carciofi e fave

This is a wonderful dish from the Ragusa province, combining four of spring's most cherished foods: baby artichokes, broad/fava beans, tiny peas and tender spring veal.

4 baby artichokes

freshly squeezed juice of 1 lemon

6 tablespoons olive oil

125 g/¾ cup fresh peas

225 g/2 cups shelled broad/fava beans

250 g/9 oz. minced/ground veal

2 tablespoons freshly grated Parmesan cheese

1 thick slice of stale country-style bread, crusts removed, soaked in milk for 15 minutes and squeezed dry

1 garlic clove, crushed

1 UK large/US extra large egg, lightly beaten

Italian '00' flour, for dredging

sea salt and freshly ground black pepper

fresh mint, chopped, to garnish

Serves 4

Remove and discard the artichoke top outer leaves and slice off the spiny tips. Remove the choke and cut the artichoke into 'Y' shapes. Put in a bowl, cover with water and add the lemon juice.

Heat 3 tablespoons of the olive oil in a medium-sized saucepan over low heat. Add the peas, broad/fava beans and artichokes. Season with salt and pepper. Stir well, cover and cook for 10 minutes, adding a few tablespoons of water to create a little steam. This is called cooking in 'umido', which preserves colour and texture.

Meanwhile, put the veal, cheese, bread, garlic and egg and seasoning in a bowl and mix well. Using your hands, form sausages the size of wine corks and dredge in flour. Heat the remaining oil in a frying pan/skillet, add the sausages and cook for 12 minutes, turning to brown on all sides.

Add the sausages to the vegetables, and stir well to blend the flavours. Garnish with freshly chopped mint and serve.

Sardine rolls stuffed with pine nut pesto

Sarde a beccafico

This is a traditional Good Friday dish in Sicily. It comes from Trapani, home of the sweetest sardines on the island. Ask your fishmonger to clean the fish if you prefer.

4 tablespoons olive oil

100 g/1¼ cups dried breadcrumbs

50 g/⅓ cup (dark) raisins, soaked in warm water for 20 minutes and squeezed dry

8 salt-packed anchovies, rinsed and finely chopped

a generous handful of flat-leaf parsley, freshly chopped

100 g/¾ cup pine nuts, finely chopped

750 g/1 lb. 10 oz. sardines, scaled, gutted, heads removed, opened flat and patted dry

3 fresh bay leaves, halved

sea salt and freshly ground black pepper

Serves 4

Preheat the oven to 180°C (350°F) Gas 4.

Heat half the olive oil in a frying pan/skillet and gently toast the breadcrumbs until they are golden brown. Set aside, reserving 2 tablespoons for sprinkling prior to cooking.

In a bowl, add the raisins, anchovies, breadcrumbs, parsley, pine nuts, salt and pepper and mix until well blended.

Place about 1 teaspoon of this mixture on each sardine, roll into a ball tail-side up and fasten with a cocktail stick/toothpick. Arrange on a baking sheet, sprinkle over the remaining breadcrumbs and oil and place a piece of bay leaf between the rolls.

Bake in the preheated oven for 30 minutes, then cool for 5 minutes before serving.

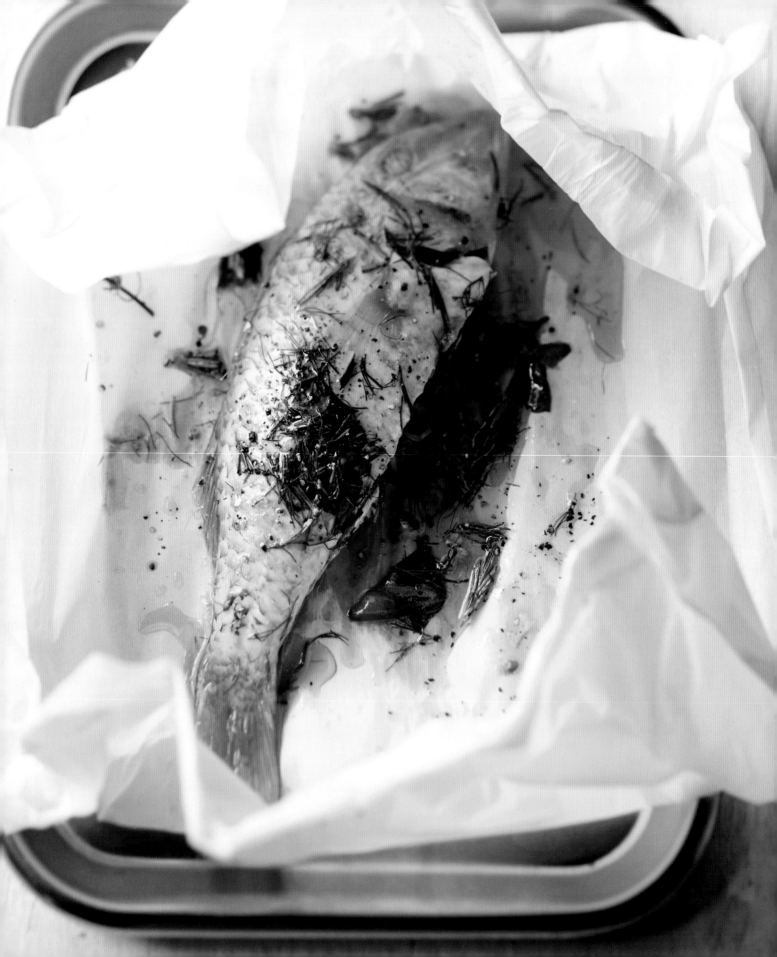

Red mullet in an envelope

Triglia alla cartocchio

Baking red mullet in a sealed parchment parcel is an excellent way of retaining the delicate flavour and enticing aroma as it cooks. The flavour is further enhanced by topping the fish with a piquant anchovy butter before baking. Ask your fishmonger to scale and gut the fish, leaving the liver in if possible as this adds to the flavour. If you can't find red mullet, grey mullet will do, or other such fish with fine white flesh.

4 red mullet, 200 g/7 oz. each
(ask your fishmonger to scale, clean
and gut them for you)

4 herb fennel sprigs

a large handful of fresh basil

1 tablespoon rosemary leaves

2 tablespoons olive oil

sea salt and freshly ground black pepper

ANCHOVY BUTTER
200 g/1¾ sticks unsalted butter,
softened

8 anchovy fillets in oil, drained

Serves 4

Preheat the oven to 200°C (400°F) Gas 6.

For the anchovy butter, put the softened butter into a bowl, add the anchovy fillets and mash together with a fork. Divide it into 4 pieces and chill until ready to use.

Rinse and dry the fish well and put some of the herbs into the cavity. Cut 4 rectangles of parchment paper large enough to envelop the fish. Brush the fish with olive oil and then place in the centre of a parchment rectangle. Add a piece of anchovy butter to each fish.

Spoon more herbs on top of the fish and season with salt and pepper. Bring the long edges of the paper up over the fish and fold together firmly. Twist the ends of the paper to seal. Place the packages on a baking sheet and bake in the preheated oven for 20 minutes.

Serve the fish in their fragrant packages.

Palermitan roasted hake

Nascello alla palermitano

To celebrate La Festa di San Pietro (St Peter's Day), residents of Palermo enjoy this dish in particular. This recipe is dedicated to Antonia, my little girl, who loves whole fish and as a very small child demanded 'fish with eyes' for her supper! Enlist the services of a fishmonger to clean the fish if needed.

5 tablespoons olive oil

4 sprigs of fresh rosemary

4 whole hake (approx. 225 g/8 oz. each), scaled, gutted, fins removed

6 salt-packed anchovies, roughly chopped

2 tablespoons freshly chopped rosemary

2 tablespoons dried breadcrumbs

sea salt and freshly ground black pepper

1 unwaxed lemon, thinly sliced, to garnish

Serves 4

Preheat the oven to 180°C (350°F) Gas 4. Oil a large baking sheet with olive oil.

Roll the rosemary sprigs in oil and place one inside the cavity of each hake. Season each fish with salt and pepper inside and out and place in a single layer on the baking sheet.

Heat 2 tablespoons of oil in a frying pan/skillet over low heat. Add the anchovies and cook until they have dissolved. Pour over the fish and sprinkle with the chopped rosemary and breadcrumbs.

Bake for 25 minutes in the preheated oven.

Place the lemon slices on top, drizzle over the remaining oil and serve.

Trapanesi couscous fish stew

Cuscus trapanese

A true sign of Africa's influence on Sicilian cooking, couscous is semolina that has been steamed and rolled into long balls. Its excellent ability to hold flavours makes it an ideal accompaniment for fish.

700 g/1 lb. 9 oz. firm, non-oily fish fillets (e.g. monkfish, sea bass, grouper, hake)

300 g/10½ oz. prawns/shrimp, calamari or lobster tail, or a mixture of all three

3 tablespoons olive oil

2 garlic cloves

500 g/3 cups fresh tomatoes, peeled and chopped

a handful of flat-leaf parsley, freshly chopped, plus extra to garnish

3 fresh bay leaves

400 g/2⅓ cups plain couscous

good-quality extra virgin olive oil

sea salt and freshly ground black pepper

Serves 4-6

Cut the fish into large pieces. Separate the tentacles of the calamari (if using) from the body, remove the heads and cut the bodies into rings.

Heat the oil in a large saucepan over medium heat, add the garlic, tomatoes and parsley and lightly cook. Add the fish, bay leaves and enough water to cover. Cook gently for 12–15 minutes.

Meanwhile, prepare the couscous. Place the couscous in a bowl and add 280 ml/1 cup plus 2 tablespoons water.) Cover the couscous with a clean dish towel and allow the grains to swell, approximately 15 minutes. Stir through 1 tablespoon of good-quality extra virgin olive oil.

Place the couscous on a platter and pour over the fish stew. Garnish with parsley and adjust the seasoning if required.

The fish of Sicily

ABOVE Sea stacks and the old tuna fishery at Scopello, near Palermo in north-west Sicily.

ABOVE RIGHT The old fish market in the crowded Piazza Alonzo di Benedetto in Catania, on Sicily's east coast.

Fishing is one of Sicily's most important industries. Surrounded by three seas (the Ionian, Tyrrhenian and Mediterranean), the islanders have always taken advantage of the rich quantity and quality of the local fish and there are still significant tuna, swordfish, sardine and anchovy fisheries around the island. However, after decades of overfishing and with the efficacy of modern fishing methods, fish stocks have declined and many of the traditions involved with fishing have dwindled too.

However, if you visit one of the many fish markets around the island, you wouldn't believe that there was a shortage at all. Stall after stall holds swathes of red prawns or tentacled squid in regimented lines. At Catania market, fish caught in the waters between there and Tunisia (which is visible on a good day) are on display: tuna, sardines, anchovies, with blue buckets of ice

keeping shellfish fresh, and ricci di mare – sea urchins – being opened prior to sale (perfect with bread and a squeeze of lemon). At Mazara del Vallo, on the same coastline and one of the most important fishing centres in Italy, huge chunks of tuna and swordfish await surgery, and the sound of hatchets on wooden boards is as characteristic of an Italian fish market as the constant shouting of vendors praising their wares. The same is true for Ortygia market and Vucciria market in Palermo where, amongst a huge choice of fish and seafood, you can buy freshly cooked octopus.

For hundreds of years (perhaps even thousands, as it is thought the Arabs introduced the concept), fishermen in Sicily have used nets to capture the bluefin tuna. This process is known as the mattanza, and it takes place in May and June when the giant fish make their way back to the Atlantic from their spawning grounds in the Mediterranean. Many small boats, from which a series of vast nets are lowered into the water, surround a school of fish, and with a succession of nets, which gradually become smaller in size,

the fish are trapped, brought to the surface and speared. (It is such a bloody business that the term mattanza in local parlance has become synonymous with 'massacre'.) Bluefin are now an endangered species, and other varieties of tuna, such as albacore, are more sustainable.

Swordfish are the other large fish caught in Sicilian waters. Special boats, known as passerelle, have a spotter (and pilot) in a tower on top and a harpoonist on a 45-metre (150-foot) metal bridge extending from the bow; when a fish is spotted, the boat slowly approaches, and the fish is speared. Swimming in pairs, swordfish travel from the Atlantic to the Tyrrhenian Sea in spring to mate. The fishermen target the female first – she is usually larger – and once she is caught, they can catch the male as well, as he will not leave her. Ironically, if the male is caught first, the female is not so loyal and usually makes her speedy escape, leaving her partner to his fate. This has been the subject of many a Sicilian folk song!

Tuna and swordfish are grilled, fried, baked or eaten as spiedini (on skewers); both can be served in carpaccio, thinly sliced, eaten raw. A famous swordfish dish is involtini di pesce spada, thin slices spread with a savoury mixture, then rolled and braised in a tomato sauce.

Sardines and anchovies are major catches in Sicilian waters, and most are used by the canning industry, which still thrives on the island. Apart, that is, from the world's first ever tuna-canning factory, opened in the 1850s in Favignana, in the Egadi Islands (a few miles west of Trapani); the factory building still dominates the small harbour, but it has been transformed into a museum dedicated to the tuna.

Fish are also salted in Sicily, making good use of the local salt from the pans in Trapani; anchovies are salted, as is grey mullet or tuna roe, for the famous dish of bottarga.

Sardines are much celebrated in Sicily, and are eaten fresh, usually in the best-known Sicilian dish, pasta con le sardine. A speciality of Palermo, this is short pasta served with a sardine and wild fennel sauce, with some classic Arabic flavourings such as pine nuts and sultanas. Sardines are also stuffed with raisins, pine nuts and breadcrumbs flavoured with orange juice – a defining flavour of Sicily – and baked. Revealing an Arabic influence, from the days when the Arabs ruled Sicily, is a famous Sicilian fish couscous, in which a variety of local fish contribute their flavours to an intense fish broth – and the fish are then thrown away!

ABOVE The mattanza is a traditional method used for netting fish.

TOP LEFT The day's catch, carefully laid out on boxes of ice in the market.

ABOVE LEFT Fishing for squid from a small boat just off the Sicilian coast.

Tuna carpaccio with lemon parsley sauce

Carpaccio di tonno

This delicious treatment of tuna can also be used with sea bass and swordfish.
I recommend getting to know your fishmonger as he or she will be able to slice the
fresh fish very thinly for you – an opportunity to show off! This dish is enjoyed in the
town of Marsala, where the fish is sweet.

400 g/14 oz. fresh tuna, cut into very
thin slices

4 tablespoons extra virgin olive oil
(not too fruity)

freshly squeezed juice of 2 lemons

sea salt and freshly ground black pepper

1 tablespoon freshly chopped oregano

2 tablespoons freshly chopped flat-leaf
parsley

250 g/9 oz. rocket/arugula, spinach or
chicory/endive (or a mixture of all three)

1 unwaxed lemon, sliced, to garnish

Serves 4

Place the tuna on a plate. Whisk together the oil, lemon
juice, salt, pepper, oregano and parsley until emulsified.

Pour the sauce over the tuna. Cover and refrigerate for
1–2 hours, turning once during that period.

Arrange the leaves on a platter, top with tuna and
serve garnished with lemon slices.

Sicilian stuffed tuna with cherry tomato sauce

Pesce tonnoripieno alla siciliana

Tuna is found in abundance in the waters around Sicily, and it is served in a variety of ways. Here the influence is definitely Arabian, with capers, spices, dried fruits and nuts.

2 tuna steaks, about 5 cm/2 inches thick

2 tablespoons (dark) raisins

2 tablespoons pine nuts

4 tablespoons dry white wine

4 tablespoons fish stock

250 g/9 oz. coarse Italian bread, crusts removed, cut into 2.5-cm/1-inch cubes

3 anchovy fillets, mashed

4 tablespoons fennel fronds, coarsely chopped

1 tablespoon plus 1 teaspoon salted capers, drained and rinsed

a pinch of ground cinnamon

a pinch of freshly grated nutmeg

sea salt and freshly ground black pepper

olive oil, for frying

Italian '00' plain flour, for dredging

a pinch of crushed dried chilli/chile (peperoncino)

400 g/2½ cups cherry tomatoes, quartered

200 g/1 cup canned chopped tomatoes

100 g/1 cup Gaeta olives, stoned/pitted and coarsely chopped

Serves 4

On a work surface, cut the tuna steaks in half crosswise, then cut each horizontally into four slices measuring 13 x 7.5 cm/ 5 x 3 inches. Cover each slice with clingfilm/plastic wrap and gently pound the slices until they are 3 mm/⅛ inch thick. Cover and refrigerate.

Soak the raisins in hot water until softened, about 10 minutes, then drain. In a small frying pan/skillet, toast the pine nuts, shaking the pan until lightly browned, about 2 minutes.

Pour the wine and fish stock into a shallow dish, add the bread and soak for about 10 minutes. Gently squeeze the bread almost dry. Finely chop the bread and transfer to a bowl. Gently stir in two-thirds of the raisins, pine nuts and anchovy fillets, half the fennel fronds and capers, and the cinnamon and nutmeg. Season to taste with salt and pepper.

Lay the tuna slices on the work surface and season with salt and pepper. Spoon 1 tablespoon of the filling into the centre of each slice and roll up like a cigar, folding the sides in as you go. Secure each roll with a wooden cocktail stick/toothpick.

Pour olive oil into a frying pan/skillet to a depth of 1 cm/½ inch. Lightly dredge the tuna rolls with flour. Fry four of the rolls at a time over moderately high heat until golden brown, about 2 minutes each side, then transfer to a plate. Repeat with the remaining rolls. Wipe out the pan with paper towels.

In the same pan heat 2 tablespoons of olive oil, add the chilli/ chile, the remaining anchovy fillet and capers, and cook for 30 seconds. Add the cherry tomatoes and canned tomatoes and cook over low heat until thickened, about 15 minutes. Stir in the olives, 1 tablespoon of the fennel fronds and the remaining pine nuts and raisins. Season with salt and pepper.

Add the tuna rolls to the sauce. Cover and simmer over low heat, turning the rolls a few times until heated through, about 3 minutes. Transfer the rolls to serving plates, remove the cocktail sticks/toothpicks and spoon the sauce on top. Garnish with the remaining fennel fronds. Serve immediately.

Breads

Pane

Semolina mountain bread with sesame seeds

Pane rimacinati

This loaf is firm and dense, but soft and chewy at the same time! Semolina – also known as durum flour – creates a wonderful flavour that I truly enjoy as my everyday bread.

15 g/½ oz. fresh yeast or 2 teaspoons dried/active dry yeast

175 ml/¾ cup warm water (37°C/99°F)

500 g/3 cups semolina (fine ground), plus extra for dusting

1½ teaspoons fine sea salt

125 ml/½ cup olive oil

egg glaze, made by mixing 1 egg yolk and 1 tablespoon water

4 tablespoons sesame seeds

Makes 2 loaves

Dissolve the fresh yeast with 100 ml/7 tablespoons of the warm water. If using dried yeast, mix with the flour.

Mix the semolina and salt together in a large bowl. Make a well in the semolina and add the olive oil and dissolved yeast. Stir in the remaining water to form a stiff sticky dough.

Turn out onto a floured work surface and knead the dough for 10 minutes until it is smooth and elastic.

Put the dough into a clean bowl, cover and leave to rise in a warm place until doubled in size, approximately 2 hours. Knock back the dough (i.e. release the gas in the dough by punching it gently), re-knead, and place the dough back in the bowl for another hour.

Knock back once more, then leave to rest for 10 minutes. Divide the dough into two pieces.

On a lightly floured work surface, shape each dough piece into an 18-cm/7-inch round. Place the dough rounds on oiled baking sheets and leave to prove until doubled in size, approximately 35 minutes.

Preheat the oven to 200°C (400°F) Gas 6.

Brush the tops of the dough rounds with egg glaze and sprinkle with sesame seeds.

Bake in the preheated oven for 30 minutes until golden brown and hollow sounding when tapped underneath. Cool on a wire rack.

Olive, rosemary and sausage bread

Pane con le olive e con la salsiccia

The Greek influence on Sicilian bread is evident in the form of sesame seeds that are sprinkled over the crust. This creates a wonderful texture and flavour, and after many visits to Sicily, I have now adopted this practice. This bread is from Agrigento, a city renowned for its archaeological site, the Valle dei Templi (Valley of the Temples).

750 g/5½ cups white strong/bread flour or a blend of spelt and wholemeal/whole-wheat (if using the latter, you'll need a little more water)

2 teaspoons sea salt

3 tablespoons olive oil

25 g/1 oz. fresh yeast or 12.5 g/½ oz. dried/active dry yeast

400 ml/1⅓ cups warm water (37°C/99°F)

175 g/1½ cups good-quality green and black olives, stoned/pitted and chopped

2 sprigs of fresh rosemary, finely chopped

175 g/6 oz. salami (preferably in a large chunk from a deli counter), chopped into 1-cm/½-inch cubes

1 egg yolk, beaten with a pinch of salt, to glaze the loaves

a generous handful of sesame seeds, for the topping

Makes 2 loaves

In a large bowl mix the flour and salt together. If you are using dried yeast, mix it with the flour. Make a well in the flour and pour in 2 tablespoons of olive oil.

Dissolve the fresh yeast in a little of the warm water and add a little of the mixture to the well. Add the rest, little by little, with a wooden spoon until a soft, craggy dough forms.

Tip the dough onto a lightly floured work surface. Knead steadily for a good 10 minutes to develop the gluten. The dough should have a beautifully marble-smooth, elastic texture.

Place the dough in a lightly oiled clean bowl. Cover with a damp, clean dish towel and allow to rise in a warm room (not too hot, as the dough will rise too quickly and won't develop a good flavour) for 1½ hours until the dough has doubled in bulk.

When the dough has doubled in bulk, knock it back (i.e. release the gas in the dough by punching it gently), then punch the dough. It will return to its original size. Add all the goodies now, i.e. olives, rosemary and salami. Knead in the added ingredients well.

Divide the dough into 2 equal rounds (I usually weigh the dough). Knead each into a ball and leave to rise again on a baking sheet, covered with a damp dish towel. The second rise should take 1 hour.

Preheat the oven to 200°C (400°F) Gas 6.

Make 3 slashes on the top of each loaf, brush over the egg yolk with salt and liberally sprinkle with sesame seeds.

Bake in the preheated oven for 25–30 minutes until the loaves have a golden crust and sound hollow when tapped underneath. Leave on a wire rack to cool.

Cool completely before devouring with good oil.

Folded parsley pizza

Calzone di prezzemolo

The literal translation of calzone is 'trouser leg', referring to the double thickness of fabric or, in this case, bread dough. The recipe comes from the Bar Mundial in Cassibile, so thank you, Gianni Fronterre. It is lighter than you might expect, not as doughy as many other calzoni, and the filling, despite being incredibly simple, is quite delicious.

7 g/¼ oz. fresh yeast or 1 teaspoon dried/active dry yeast

1 teaspoon caster/superfine sugar

225–250 ml/¾–1 cup warm water (37°C/99°F)

550 g/4 cups white strong/bread flour, plus extra for dusting

1 tablespoon salt

100 ml/7 tablespoons olive oil

1 onion, finely chopped

a very large handful of flat-leaf parsley, freshly chopped

350 g/12 oz. mozzarella cheese, cut into small cubes

freshly ground black pepper

Makes 1 large calzone

Cream the yeast with the sugar and a little of the water. If using dried yeast, mix it with the flour.

Mix the flour and salt in a large bowl. Add half the oil and the creamed yeast together with the remaining water. Mix with a wooden spoon to form a ragged dough.

Turn out of the bowl and knead vigorously for 10 minutes until soft and pliable. Return the soft dough to a clean bowl. Cover with a damp, clean dish towel and leave to rise in a warm place until doubled in size, about 1 hour.

Meanwhile, prepare the filling. Heat the remaining oil in a frying pan/skillet. Fry the onion until soft, then add the parsley and stir for 2 minutes over medium heat. Season with pepper and leave to one side. When cool, mix in the cheese.

Preheat the oven to 200°C (400°F) Gas 6.

Knock back the dough (i.e. release the gas in the dough by punching it gently) and knead for 4 minutes. Roll out into a large rectangle 38 x 20 cm/15 x 8 inches. Spread the onion and cheese mixture over the dough, leaving a 1-cm/½-inch margin all round.

Fold the dough lengthways into three, enclosing the filling, and place on a greased baking sheet. Leave for 10 minutes to rise again, then dust with flour.

Bake in the preheated oven for 20 minutes until light and golden. Cool on a wire rack, then cut into thick or thin slices and serve hot, cold or warm as snacks or canapés.

The breads of Sicily

Bread is important throughout Italy, but in Sicily it is sacrosanct. The English word 'company' comes from the Latin *con pane*, meaning 'with bread'. And to Sicilians, to bake and break bread with family and friends – in companionship – is one of the fundamental needs and pleasures of life, giving nourishment to both body and soul. Bread is a staple of the Sicilian diet.

TOP ROW LEFT Cucciddati – bread prepared for the feast of St Joseph in Calatafimi, near Trapani.

TOP ROW CENTRE Santa Lucia, who is celebrated on 13th December.

TOP ROW RIGHT Cuddure - Easter doughnuts.

CENTRE RIGHT A large tray of pizza with a generous topping, ready for baking.

BOTTOM ROW LEFT Semolina bread. The dough is shaped into a circle and slashed with a knife before backing.

BOTTOM ROW RIGHT Distributing bread at the feast of San Paolo in Palazzolo Acreide, in south-eastern Sicily.

Sicily was once known as the bread basket of the Roman Empire, as the island produced so much good-quality wheat. During the Arab rule, from the 9th to the 11th centuries AD, wheat production continued, and many early texts mention *semola* (or semolina, a flour made from durum wheat) being dried and cooked in strands. With its ideal climate, for both growing and drying, Sicily might indeed have been where pasta originated!

This same *semola* that perhaps made the first Italian pasta is used in Sicily's most traditional bread. The durum wheat kernels are ground coarsely to a texture like cornmeal, then ground again to make a finer bread flour, known as *rimacinata*. This flour is mixed with water, salt and yeast, with no fat added at all. This combination, with its high content of gluten, produces a golden bread, with an aerated texture and a distinct chewiness. It is often baked in wood-burning stoves (sometimes fired with almond shells), and has a delicious crust. Curiously, this golden chewy bread exists now only in the countryside; in the cities, ordinary wheat flour, shortened with fat, is now used to make a more delicate white bread.

Sicilian breads can be shaped into familiar batons, into large rounds, crescents, *occhi* or 'eyes' (like a scrolled S), or the serpent-like coils of *mafalda*, all of which may be topped with sesame seeds before baking. At Easter in Sicily, as in the rest of Italy, special breads are baked and served at Easter lunch, or to be taken on traditional countryside picnics or *scampagnata*. Bread (or biscuit/cookie) dough is formed into many shapes – circles, wreaths, rabbits, flowers, braids, doves,

baskets, nests – and painted hard-boiled eggs, still in their shells, are often included in the dough before baking. These eggs are the symbol of fertility and new beginnings, and in Italy have long been a tradition at Easter.

An interesting Sicilian bread is *pane squaratu*, which is boiled before it is baked. It is usually formed into a ring with four rosettes and flavoured with aniseed. At home, after baking, a fresh warm loaf is halved and sandwiched with olive oil, cherry tomatoes, grated Pecorino and basil; after a brief 'marination', this *pane cunzato* is cut into thick slices. For special occasions, many *focaccia*-like breads and pizzas are stuffed before baking.

Although one associates Italy with 'slow food', Palermo, the capital of Sicily, is said to be the fifth best city in the world for street food, and much of this food is based on bread dough. *Sfincione* is a rustic bread base, topped with a variety of ingredients (usually tomatoes, onions, olive oil, cheese and anchovies), before being baked. Another Palermo street speciality is *pane con la milza*, a soft roll filled with fried calf spleen, lung and liver, sprinkled with lemon juice; for the *maritata* (married) version, the offal is topped with grated Caciocavallo cheese. Another, rather more substantial, offering is *pane con panelle e cazzilli*: panelle (chickpea pancakes) and *cazzilli* (potato croquettes) are combined in a soft roll.

In the mid 1700s the Sicilian wheat harvest failed. The resulting famine led to riots and people prayed to the local saint, Santa Lucia, for deliverance. Legend has it that on 13th December one year, a storm forced a ship into Syracuse harbour. It was laden with wheat and in gratitude to the saint, the Sicilians swore not to eat bread or pasta on that day, now the saint's day. Instead they ate *cuccia* (boiled whole wheat kernels) or *arancini* (fried rice balls). Towns in Sicily have festivals to celebrate the day, and in Paceco, near Trapani, a modern replica of the 'providence ship' is driven through the streets, handing out *cuccia*. Many Italian-Americans also abstain from eating wheat on St Lucy's Day, and I have heard that in Texas *arancini* stuffed with *chilli con carne* are served, a true example of fusion food!

Sicilian stuffed pizza

Pizza ripieno alla siciliano

This is a popular pizza enjoyed over the whole of the island. With its simple and hearty ingredients, this qualifies as the ultimate comfort food.

PIZZA DOUGH

250 g/2 scant cups white strong/bread flour

1 teaspoon fine sea salt

2 tablespoons olive oil

10 g/½ oz. fresh yeast, crumbled, or
1 teaspoon dried/active dry yeast

50–75 ml/3–5 tablespoons water at body temperature (water quantity will vary depending on surrounding temperature and freshness of the flour)

FILLING

1 medium aubergine/eggplant, peeled and diced

fine sea salt and freshly ground black pepper

3 tablespoons olive oil

1 small onion, finely chopped

150 g/5½ oz. minced/ground pork

1 garlic clove, finely chopped

7 fresh tomatoes, seeded and chopped

1 tablespoon tomato purée/paste

2 generous pinches of dried oregano

Serves 3

For the pizza dough, mix the flour and salt in a large bowl. If using dried yeast, mix it with the flour. Make a well in the middle and add the oil. Dissolve the yeast in some of the water and add into the well. Mix and keep adding the rest of the water, little by little, and the result should be a damp, raggy dough – this stage is very important.

Tip the dough out onto a lightly floured surface and knead for 10 minutes. Shape it into a ball and place in an oiled bowl. Cover with a damp dish towel and leave to rise for 1 hour (the slow rise gives more flavour). It should double in size. Knock back (i.e. release the gas in the dough by punching it gently) and knead for 10 minutes. Leave for a further 2 hours.

Meanwhile, make the filling. Spread the aubergine/eggplant pieces out in one layer on a baking sheet. Sprinkle with salt and weigh down with another baking sheet. Leave for 10 minutes. Rinse, drain and pat the aubergine/eggplant slices dry with paper towels.

Heat the oil in a medium frying pan/skillet over medium heat and cook the onion until it is softened but not brown, about 2 minutes. Add the pork and cook until it is slightly brown, about 4–5 minutes. Add the aubergine/eggplant and garlic and cook for a further 4–5 minutes, stirring frequently. Add the tomatoes, tomato purée/ paste, oregano and some salt and pepper to taste. Cook for 20 minutes on low heat.

Preheat the oven to 200°C (400°F) Gas 6 at least 30 minutes prior to baking. If you have a pizza stone, place in the oven to preheat.

Knead the knocked-back dough on a lightly floured surface for 2–3 minutes, then divide the dough into 6 pieces to a thickness of 1 cm/½ inch and a diameter of 25 cm/10 inches. Place three of the rounds on a flour-dusted pizza paddle or a baking sheet. Spread some of the filing in the centre of each pizza, leaving a 1 cm/½ inch rim. Top with another round of dough and pinch the edges to seal. With a sharp knife, make three slashes in the top and brush well with a little olive oil.

Slide the three pizzas onto the pizza stone and bake in the preheated oven for 20 minutes or until the edges are golden brown. Remove from the oven, cut in half and serve at once.

Anchovy and mozzarella mini rolls

Crispeddi siciliani

Since Sicily is known as the bread basket of the Mediterranean, I am always delighted by such interesting and varied styles of bread wherever I travel around this magical island. These wonderfully crisp rolls are really fun to make and eat and feature in Agrigento wheat festival celebrations every spring. Be adventurous with the filling as different herb and cheese combinations work well. I think they are great to take to picnics or as canapés. My daughter loves it when I serve them at her birthday parties.

250 g/2 cups minus 2 tablespoons white strong/bread flour

2 teaspoons fine sea salt

10 g/2 teaspoons fresh yeast, crumbled or 1 teaspoon dried/active dry yeast

2 tablespoons olive oil

150 ml/⅔ cup water, at body temperature

12 anchovies, chopped

125 g/4½ oz. buffalo mozzarella, chopped

a handful of flat-leaf parsley, freshly chopped

Makes 12

In a large bowl mix the flour and salt together. If using dried yeast, mix it with the flour. Make a well in the centre and add the oil. Dissolve the yeast in one-third of the water and add to the well in the flour. Using a wooden spoon, add enough of the remaining water to form a firm but damp dough.

Turn the dough out onto a lightly floured surface and knead for 10 minutes. Place in a lightly oiled bowl, cover with a damp dish towel and leave to rise for 1 hour. After 1 hour, knock back the dough (i.e. release the gas in the dough by punching it gently) and knead again for 5 minutes to relax it. Cover the dough and leave to rest for another 5 minutes.

Divide the rested dough into 12 little balls. Flatten each in the palm of your hand and fill it with the chopped anchovy, mozzarella and parsley and pinch it closed into a ball, enclosing the filling. Put the little balls on a greased baking sheet, seam-side down, cover and leave to prove for 20 minutes.

Preheat the oven to 200°C (400°F) Gas 6.

Bake the rolls for 12–15 minutes in the preheated oven until they are golden. Cool slightly on a wire rack, and eat while still warm.

TIP You may like to roll the balls in a little semolina to create a crisp texture on the outside.

Desserts

Dolci e pasticceria

Almond pastries

Fior di mandorlia

The Arab influence in Sicily is very distinctive. This recipe illustrates this point, as cinnamon is of Arab origin. This particular pastry is found around Agrigento. Excellent for gluten and wheat intolerances, but simply divine all the same.

200 g/2 cups freshly ground almonds

50 g/3 tablespoons fragrant honey

100 g/½ cup caster/granulated sugar

1 teaspoon ground cinnamon

grated zest of 1 unwaxed lemon

¼ teaspoon freshly grated nutmeg

¼ teaspoon allspice

1 egg white (UK large/US extra large)

1 teaspoon pure vanilla extract

icing/confectioners' sugar, for dusting

Makes 18

Preheat the oven to 150°C (300°F) Gas 2.

Mix all the ingredients together, then knead until the oils from the almonds are released into the pastry.

Shape into smooth cakes 3 cm/1¼ inches in diameter. Place onto a parchment-lined baking sheet and bake for 20–25 minutes.

Cool on a wire rack, then dust generously with icing/confectioners' sugar.

Cinnamon buns with pistachio cream filling

Panini dolci alla canella con pistacchio piene de crema

The use of cinnamon is extensive in Sicilian cusine and the pistachio filling used here is simply delicious paired with it. These buns are good for breakfast, brunch or a mid-afternoon pick-me-up.

135 g/⅔ cup caster/granulated sugar

100 g/7 tablespoons unsalted butter

700 g/6½ cups Italian '00' flour

a generous pinch of salt

7 g/¼ oz. fresh yeast or 7g/1 teaspoon dried/active dry yeast

1 UK large/US extra large egg

200 ml/¾ cup whole milk

100 ml/7 tablespoons single/light cream

1 tablespoon ground cinnamon

PISTACHIO CREAM FILLING

90 g/½ cup caster/granulated sugar

125 g/1 cup whole, shelled unsalted pistachios

100 g/7 tablespoons unsalted butter

TO GLAZE

1 egg, beaten

50 ml/3 tablespoons golden/light corn syrup, mixed with 1 tablespoon warm water

2 tablespoons caster/granulated sugar

Makes 16

To make the pistachio cream filling, blend all the ingredients in a food processor until smooth and creamy. Set aside.

For the dough, beat together the sugar and butter for 3 minutes until light and fluffy. Mix the flour and salt in a separate bowl (if using dried yeast, mix with the flour). Add the yeast to a bowl with around 2 tablespoons warm water. Allow it to dissolve and mix a little.

Add the egg to the butter mixture and beat for 2 minutes, gradually adding the milk, cream, flour, the yeast mixture and the cinnamon. Mix well. It should be slightly sticky. Knead for 10 minutes, adding a little more flour if necessary. Put in a clean bowl, cover with a damp dish towel and leave in a warm place for 1 hour until it has doubled in size.

Shape the risen dough into a rough rectangle and roll out to the thickness of 2 cm/¾ inch. Spread the pistachio cream over the dough. Fold the dough in half, then in half again, keeping the rectangular shape. Roll it out again until it's approximately 1.5 cm/½ inch thick. Cut the dough into long strips, about 2 cm/¾ inch wide. You should make 16.

Roll the strips of dough into snail shapes. Place on a baking sheet lined with parchment paper. Cover with a clean damp dish towel and allow the buns to rise for 45 minutes.

Preheat the oven to 200°C (400°F) Gas 6.

Brush the buns with beaten egg and bake in the preheated oven for about 12 minutes, until golden. Meanwhile, prepare a sugar syrup by mixing the golden/light corn syrup mixture and sugar together.

As soon as the buns come out of the oven, brush them with the sugar syrup and leave to cool on a wire rack.

Apricot custard fritters

Albicocche fritte

This is classic Sicilian street food to enjoy in spring when apricots are plentiful. I enjoyed these with my mother in Messina many, many years ago.

180 g/scant 1½ cups Italian '00' flour

1 tablespoon golden caster/granulated sugar

2 UK large/US extra large eggs, separated

180 ml/¾ cup lager, at room temperature

60 g/½ stick unsalted butter, melted

4 apricots, halved and stoned/pitted

groundnut oil, for frying

icing/confectioners' sugar, for dusting

VANILLA CUSTARD

600 ml/2⅓ cups whole milk

1 vanilla pod/bean, split

140 g/¾ cup golden caster/granulated sugar

120 g/1 scant cup Italian '00' flour

60 g/¾ cup unsalted butter

5 egg yolks

Makes 8

For the vanilla custard, bring the milk, vanilla pod/bean and 40 g/3 tablespoons sugar to the boil in a saucepan over medium-high heat. Place the flour, butter and remaining sugar in a mixing bowl and using fingertips, rub the mixture together until it resembles breadcrumbs. Whisk in the milk mixture until smooth, return to the saucepan and stir continuously over low heat until thick and the flour cooks, approximately 6 minutes.

Remove from the heat, remove the vanilla pod/bean, then whisk in the yolks. Cover the surface with parchment paper to stop a skin forming and refrigerate until cold.

Heat the oil in a large deep saucepan. In a bowl combine the flour and sugar, make a well in the centre, add the yolks and lager and whisk to combine, then stir in the melted butter. In a separate bowl, whisk the egg whites until stiff and gently fold into the batter.

Mould the cold custard around the apricot halves, dip into the batter and fry in batches, turning until golden brown, around 4 minutes.

Drain on paper towels and serve hot, dusted with icing/confectioners' sugar.

Chocolate cherry amaretti

Cioccolato amaretti

These wonderful little treats are very noticeable in pasticceria (confectioners' shops), particularly in Syracusa. I think they're best made 'a casa lingor' (at home).

250 g/2½ cups freshly ground almonds (for maximum flavour)

120 g/1¼ cups caster/granulated sugar

50 g/½ cup dark/bittersweet chocolate, grated

60 g/½ cup dried cherries, chopped

finely grated zest of 1 unwaxed lemon

2 UK large/US extra large egg whites

a pinch of salt

30 g/3½ tablespoons icing/confectioners' sugar

Makes 12-14

Preheat the oven to 160°C (325°F) Gas 3.

Mix the almonds, caster/granulated sugar, chocolate, cherries and lemon zest together. Whisk the egg whites until firm and add to the almond mixture with the salt. Mix well. The mixture should be damp.

Sift the icing/confectioners' sugar into a bowl. Form balls with the almond mixture, about the size of three-quarters of a tablespoon. Roll in icing/confectioners' sugar and place on a parchment-lined baking sheet.

Bake in the preheated oven until they have a golden tinge, approximately 12–14 minutes. Cool on a wire rack.

Chocolate and ricotta tart

Crostata di ricotta a cioccolato

This is a tart for celebrations. Ricotta is a wonderful carrier of flavours and the pastry cream is luxuriant. This sublime dessert was served at my Sicilian friend's wedding in Catania.

PASTRY

300 g/1½ cups Italian '00' flour, plus extra for dusting

2 UK large/US extra large eggs

1 UK large/US extra large egg yolk

100 g/½ cup golden caster/granulated sugar

2 teaspoons grated zest from an unwaxed lemon

a pinch of sea salt

125 g/1 stick plus 1 tablespoon unsalted butter

PASTRY CREAM

250 ml/1 cup whole milk

1 large piece of unwaxed lemon zest

2 UK large/US extra large egg yolks

50 g/¼ cup golden caster/granulated sugar

2 tablespoons Italian '00' flour

1 teaspoon vanilla extract

RICOTTA FILLING

300 g/10½ oz. ricotta cheese

50 g/¼ cup golden caster/granulated sugar

100 g/scant ¾ cup chopped dark/bittersweet chocolate (70% cocoa)

DECORATION

18 whole blanched almonds

18 walnut halves

vanilla icing/confectioners' sugar

28-cm/11-inch tart pan

Serves 8-10

Put all the pastry ingredients in a food processor and combine. Remove the dough and knead very lightly on a work surface, then wrap in greaseproof paper and chill for 30 minutes.

For the pastry cream, combine the milk and zest in a medium saucepan and place over low heat until just below boiling.

Blend the egg yolks and sugar in a medium bowl with a wire whisk. Add the flour and stir until it has dissolved. Slowly whisk one-third of the milk into the egg yolk mixture. Add the remaining milk all at once and blend well.

Pour the mixture back into the saucepan and return it to the heat. Stir constantly until the custard has thickened. Remove from the heat and stir in the vanilla. Continue to stir for 1 minute. Remove the lemon zest, pour the custard into a bowl and cover the surface with parchment paper to prevent a skin forming. Allow to cool.

For the ricotta filling, mix the ricotta, sugar and chocolate together well.

Preheat the oven to 200°C (400°F) Gas 6.

Put two-thirds of the pastry dough on a lightly floured surface, flour the rolling pin and roll out the pastry to a circle about 35 cm/14 inches in diameter and 5 mm/¼ inch thick. Carefully roll the dough onto the rolling pin, then lower into the tart pan. Gently press the dough against the sides of the pan.

Trim off the excess dough and roll a portion of it to a thickness of 1 cm/½ inch and 28 cm/11 inches long. Place this dough rope across the centre of the tart to divide the shell in half.

Spread the pastry cream over one half of the tart shell and the ricotta filling over the other half. Use the remaining dough to make more 1 cm/½ inch thick ropes. Arrange over the filling in a lattice pattern. Place an almond in each square over the ricotta filling and walnut halves over the pastry cream.

Bake in the centre of the preheated oven for 40–45 minutes or until the crust is golden. Cool and dust with icing/confectioners' sugar before serving.

Fig, nut and chocolate cake

Cioccolato e fico palermitano

This rich tart once more illustrates the Sicilian love of nuts and fruits. Every Sicilian market is full of stalls laden with local fruits and nuts and the ground on market days crunches underfoot with shells of the pistachios and pumpkin seeds the stallholders and their customers have enjoyed during the day. I have often thought it is this passion for nuts and seeds with their Vitamin E content that makes the skin of Sicilians so healthy and fresh looking.

PASTRY

150 g/1 stick plus 2 tablespoons unsalted butter

100 g/½ cup caster/granulated sugar

300 g/2⅓ cups Italian '00' flour, plus extra for dusting

60 ml/4 tablespoons Marsala

a pinch of sea salt

1 egg yolk (UK large/US extra large)

55 g/½ cup shelled unsalted pistachios, finely chopped

icing/confectioners' sugar, for dusting

FILLING

300 g/2 cups dried figs, chopped

30 g/¼ cup (dark) raisins

10 g/1 tablespoon whole almonds, toasted and chopped

55 g/½ cup chopped walnuts

grated zest of 2 unwaxed lemons

100 g/3½ oz dark/bittersweet chocolate (70% cocoa), chopped

60 ml/4 tablespoons dry Marsala

a pinch of ground cinnamon

Serves 8

For the pastry, in a bowl work the butter with the sugar, flour, Marsala and salt. When you have a smooth dough, wrap it in clingfilm/plastic wrap and leave to rest for 1 hour.

Make the filling by putting all the ingredients into a saucepan. Simmer over low heat for 20 minutes, stirring frequently to prevent burning. Leave to cool.

Preheat the oven to 200°C (400°F) Gas 6.

Using a rolling pin, roll the pastry dough out on a floured surface into a rectangle about 1 cm/½ inch thick. Pour the cooked and cooled filling into the centre, roll up the dough and join the edges to make a ring. Pierce the surface with the tines of a fork, place on a greased baking sheet and bake for 25–35 minutes until golden.

Beat the egg yolk. Brush the cake with the beaten yolk and sprinkle with the chopped pistachio nuts, then return to the oven for 5 minutes.

Place on a wire rack to cool. Sprinkle with icing/confectioners' sugar before serving.

Strawberry and pistachio cake

Torta di pistacchio e fragola

This is truly delicious and it will win you many gasps of approval as it looks stunning. It's best made when the strawberries are at their best, in the summer.

55 g/½ stick unsalted butter

6 UK large/US extra large eggs, beaten

140 g/¾ cup caster/granulated sugar

a few drops of pure vanilla extract

140 g/1 cup plain/all-purpose or Italian '00' flour

100 g/1 cup shelled and skinned pistachio nuts, ground

FILLING AND DECORATION

350 g/12½ oz. fresh strawberries

1 tablespoon Marsala

600 ml/2¾ cups double/heavy cream

two 20-cm/8-inch round cake pans, buttered and base-lined with baking parchment

Serves 8–12

Preheat the oven to 180°C (350°F) Gas 4.

Melt the butter in a small saucepan and leave to cool.

Put the eggs, sugar and vanilla extract in a bowl. Whisk until pale and thick enough to leave a ribbon-like trail for 8 seconds when the whisk is lifted.

Sift the flour and fold half of it into the egg mixture. Pour a little of the cooled butter around the edge of the mixture and carefully fold in 2 tablespoons of the remaining flour. Repeat, folding carefully to ensure you maintain a mousse-like consistency, until all the butter and flour are used up. Divide the mixture in half and spoon one-half into one of the prepared cake pans. Fold 25 g/2 tablespoons of the pistachio nuts into the remaining mixture and pour into the other pan.

Bake both cakes in the preheated oven for 35–40 minutes, or until they have just started shrinking from the sides of the pan. Cool in the pans for 5 minutes, then turn the cakes out onto a wire rack and leave to cool.

To fill and decorate, thinly slice the strawberries. Sprinkle the Marsala over the plain cake and then split both cakes in half horizontally. Whip the cream until it just holds its shape and divide into two portions. Set one portion aside.

Place a pistachio cake layer on a flat plate and spread over half of one portion of the cream. Add a plain cake layer, half the strawberries, another pistachio cake layer and the remaining cream. Top with the plain cake layer.

Coat the top and sides of the cake with two-thirds of the reserved cream. Lightly press the remaining pistachio nuts on the sides of the cake. Spoon the remaining cream in blobs around the top of the cake and decorate with the remaining strawberries.

Cannoli

Cannoli

Cannoli are perhaps the most famous dessert of Sicily, available everywhere on the island. They vary considerably. These pastries are traditionally made with wooden cannoli tubes which can be bought from specialist kitchen shops. Should these be difficult to find, I have adapted the recipe so that you can make them without the tubes.

The most important thing to remember when preparing cannoli is to fill cooked shells just before serving so they are very crisp and crunchy. Avoid buying from a pasticceria – they will have been filled too early and will be soggy.

CANNOLI PASTRY

25 g/2 tablespoons unsalted butter

1 egg white

55 g/¼ cup caster/granulated sugar

25 g/2 tablespoons Italian '00' flour, plus extra for dusting

1 teaspoon cocoa powder

FILLING

55 g/2 oz. ricotta

1 tablespoon caster/granulated sugar

25 g/1 oz. dark/bittersweet chocolate (70% cocoa), grated

25 g/¼ cup shelled pistachio nuts, chopped

finely grated zest of ½ unwaxed lemon

½ teaspoon pure vanilla extract

a pinch of ground cinnamon

icing/confectioners' sugar and cocoa powder, for dusting

Makes 8

Preheat the oven to 190°C (375°F) Gas 5. Grease the handles of two wooden spoons and line two baking sheets with parchment paper.

To make the pastry cases, melt the butter and leave to cool. Whisk the egg white until stiff, then fold in the sugar. Sift the flour and cocoa powder over the egg mixture and fold in. Trickle the butter around the sides of the bowl and fold in. Put 1 tablespoon of the mixture onto each of the prepared baking trays and spread to circles about 10 cm/4 inches in diameter. Repeat, making two circles per baking sheet.

Bake for 7 minutes until firm to the touch. Slide a palette knife under each circle, then wrap around the wooden spoons. Leave to cool, then ease off the handles and cool on a wire rack. Use the remaining mixture in the same way to make 8 pastry tubes.

To make the filling, put the ricotta into a small bowl and mix in the sugar, then fold the grated chocolate into the mixture with the nuts, lemon zest, vanilla and cinnamon.

Fill a piping/pastry bag with a large plain nozzle/tip with the ricotta mixture and use to stuff the pastry tubes.

Place the pastries on a serving dish and dust with icing/confectioners' sugar and cocoa powder. Serve at once.

Cassata

Cassata

450 g/1 lb. ricotta

225 g/1 cup plus 2 tablespoons caster/granulated sugar

225 g/8 oz. dark/bittersweet chocolate (70% cocoa)

½ teaspoon ground cinnamon

2 tablespoons Amaretto, or other almond-flavoured liqueur

175 g/1¾ cups shelled pistachio nuts, chopped

200 g/7 oz. glacé/candied fruits, chopped

12 Italian lady finger/savoiardi biscuits (see recipe below or use sponge fingers)

½ Italian sponge cake (see below), cut horizontally

ITALIAN LADY FINGERS

3 UK large/US extra large eggs, separated

1 teaspoon pure vanilla extract

85 g/¾ cup self-raising/rising flour

1 teaspoon baking powder

¼ teaspoon salt

85 g/¼ cup plus 2 tablespoons caster/granulated sugar

ITALIAN SPONGE CAKE

5 UK large/US extra large eggs, separated

225 g/1 cup plus 2 tablespoons caster/granulated sugar

200 g/1½ cups plain/all-purpose white or Italian '00' flour

finely grated zest of 2 unwaxed lemons

1 teaspoon pure vanilla extract

1 teaspoon rum

TOPPING

225 ml/1 cup double/heavy cream

1 tablespoon Amaretto

glacé/candied fruit, to decorate

23-cm/9-inch loose-bottomed round, deep cake pan, greased and floured

Serves 8–10

This is a simple, classic dessert, made from ricotta and sponge cake, and should not be confused with cassata gelata, which is an ice-cream bombe. Prepare it a day ahead of time.

Preheat the oven to 180°C (350°F) Gas 4.

To make the Italian lady fingers, beat the egg yolks until thick, then beat in the vanilla extract. In a bowl, sift the flour and baking powder together. Whisk the egg whites until stiff, then whisk in the salt and sugar until the whites are glossy and very stiff. Using a metal spoon, fold the egg yolks into the egg whites, followed by the sifted flour. Drop tablespoons of the batter onto an ungreased baking sheet, and spread to form fingers measuring about 20 x 6 cm (8 x 2½ inches). Bake for 10 minutes until golden. Transfer to a wire rack and leave to cool.

To make the sponge cake, whisk together the egg yolks and sugar until thick and creamy. Whisk the egg whites until stiff, then gently fold into the egg yolk mixture. Gradually sift in and fold in the flour. Add the lemon zest, vanilla and rum, and mix together until well blended. Pour the mixture into the prepared cake pan and bake for 30–35 minutes, until golden brown and well risen. Turn onto a wire rack and leave to cool.

Line the base and sides of a 1.7-litre/3-pint pudding basin with clingfilm/plastic wrap.

Beat together the ricotta and sugar until light and fluffy. Divide the mixture in half.

Chop half of the chocolate into small pieces. Add to half of the ricotta mixture with the cinnamon and Amaretto. Fold the pistachio nuts and glacé fruits through the other half. Cover both mixtures and set aside.

Use the lady fingers to line the prepared basin, pressing them firmly around the bowl so that they are even. Fill first with the fruit-ricotta mixture, then with the chocolate-ricotta mixture. Cover the top with the cake. Cover the bowl with clingfilm/plastic wrap and freeze for 2 hours or longer.

Remove the basin from the freezer. Melt the remaining chocolate and pour over the top of the sponge in the bowl. Return to the freezer for about 15 minutes, until set.

To make the topping, whip the cream and Amaretto together until it just holds its shape.

Just before serving, turn out the cassata. Ease around the edges of the basin with a palette knife, then place a serving plate over the top. Invert the basin onto the plate, and let the cassata gently ease out, chocolate side down.

Spread over the cream mixture to cover, and decorate with glacé/candied fruit.

Chocolate nougat ice cream

Semifreddo al torroncino

This gelato is the closest thing there is to Nutella ice cream and for that reason, it's most enjoyable! I tried it on a very warm April day at Mondello beach – a beautiful stretch of sand surrounded by mountains on the outskirts of Palermo – many years ago and it's stayed in my mind ever since. The town of Mondello is very attractive, with its famous Art Nouveau villas. King Ferdinand of Bourbon (1725–1825) referred to Mondello as a 'corner of paradise'.

3 UK large/US extra large eggs, separated

3 tablespoons caster/granulated sugar

300 g/10½ oz. mascarpone cheese

100 g/3½ oz. dark/bittersweet chocolate (70% cocoa), melted and cooled

100 g/3½ oz brittle nougat, chopped

75 g/½ cup toasted hazelnuts, crushed, to decorate

1-kg/2¼-lb. loaf pan lined with clingfilm/plastic wrap (pushed well into the corners and sides)

Serves 6–8

In a mixing bowl, beat the egg yolks with the sugar until pale and fluffy (approximately 8 minutes). Add the mascarpone and keep beating, then stir in the melted cooled chocolate and the chopped nougat.

In a large bowl, whisk the egg whites until floppy, then fold into the egg yolk mixture.

Pour the mixture into the prepared loaf pan and freeze for several hours.

To serve, unmould onto a serving dish, decorate with crushed toasted hazelnuts and slice or scoop into dishes. Enjoy!

Pistachio ice cream

Gelato al pistacchio rustico

I visited Palermo for research in the middle of April. I took my little girl Antonia with me and we were both hugely excited. I knew that her love of food and her honesty would provide me with excellent criticism of dishes that we encountered. Our morning in Palermo was spent visiting a bustling speciality market; by midday we were hot and tired, the sun surprising us with its strength. We made a quick decision to return to our hotel, change and head for the beautiful Mondello beach, a half-hour drive away, where we first tasted this ice cream.

Along with citrus fruits, pistachios have been granted DOP (Protected Designation of Origin) status in Sicily, with the Bronte pistachio – which is only grown in Sicily – proving to be the very best.

100 g/1 cup shelled pistachios, unsalted

450 ml/1¾ cups whole milk

450 ml/2 cups double/heavy cream

1 teaspoon pure vanilla extract

¼ teaspoon sea salt, crushed

100 g/½ cup golden caster/granulated sugar

4 UK large/US extra large eggs

Serves 4–6

Preheat the oven to 180°C (350°F) Gas 4.

Line a baking sheet with parchment paper. Spread the nuts out in a single layer and toast in the oven for 8 minutes. Cool.

Heat the milk and cream together in a saucepan until scalding.

Grind the cooled nuts in a food processor until fine but with a little texture, if you like texture. Add the vanilla and salt, and stir well.

Whisk the sugar and eggs together until thick and creamy, and the whisk leaves a trail when lifted from the bowl, approximately 8–10 minutes.

Combine the milk and eggs together in the pan and gently cook the custard mixture over low heat. This should not take longer than 8 minutes. Stir really well as this could turn to scrambled egg, so heat gently and carefully.

If you would like a pronounced green gelato, cool the mixture and leave overnight in the fridge, then freeze and churn in an ice-cream machine as per the manufacturer's instructions. If, like me, you are impatient, leave the creamy pistachio custard to cool, then freeze and churn.

Serve on its own, or with chocolate ice cream – they are rather good together.

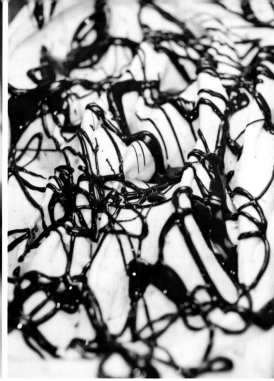

Gelateria

Ice-cream in Italy is called *gelato* (literally 'iced' or 'frozen') and the plural is *gelati* . Italian *gelati* are famed throughout the world, and *gelati* from Sicily are perhaps the most famous of all. They say that the first ice-creams were made in Ancient Greek and Roman times from snow from the slopes of Mount Etna: this snow was gathered by runners who brought it, as speedily as possible, to the cities of Taormina or Catania to be flavoured with honey, fruit – possibly Sicilian lemon pulp or purée – or nuts.

However, nobody really knows definitively where and how ice cream came into being. Some believe the idea came from China, and found its way via the Silk Route (as did so many ideas, products and foodstuffs) to the Middle East. The Arab conquerors of Sicily could well have invented ice cream there, for Sicily was to play a large part in ice cream's history. Florence's Catherine de Medici may have introduced many things to France when she went to marry the future Henry II in the early 16th century – the fork, the artichoke, petits pois and water ices, among them – but it was a Sicilian who is credited with introducing proper ice cream to Paris. One Francesco Procopio dei Coltelli opened a shop selling coffee and sorbets there in the late 17th century. He later developed what we would recognise as real ice cream, using cream, eggs and sugar. (Café Procope, the oldest restaurant in Paris, still exists, and offers ice cream on its menu to this day.)

The first ices would have been water ices, made primarily of flavoured liquid or fruit purée. As knowledge grew, and tastes changed, these water ices were transformed. When liquid is frozen, it forms hard, crunchy crystals. These crystals need to be as small as possible in order to make the ice cream smooth and palatable. By adding extra ingredients, such as sugar or fat, the crystallisation process is slowed down and inhibited. When the fat

of milk or cream – or indeed the milk and eggs of a custard – is emulsified into the base ice cream mix, it interferes with the way the water freezes, keeping the mixture softer. Sugar has much the same effect.

But why are Italian, and Sicilian, *gelati* so famous, and taste so different from other ice creams? Sorbets, water ices and *granitas* – all water-based ices – are much the same, but where the dairy- or custard-based ices are concerned, less makes for better. American and British ice creams can contain as much as 20 per cent cream; Italian ice cream is more likely to be made from less than 10 per cent cream. As the fat in milk and cream tends to coat the tongue, so it interferes with the tastebuds' abilities to taste. With the less fat-dense *gelati*, the flavours come through much more directly, giving cleaner and more intense flavours.

Most ice creams are churned, both to prevent crystals forming and to introduce air, which softens the texture. Italian ice creams are also churned, but at a much slower pace which means less air is introduced. This is why Italian ice creams are denser and milkier in texture, without the slippery softness of many other soft ice creams. Neither are they frozen hard, like many commercial ice creams; they are always served at a slightly warmer temperature.

Granita – a simple combination of sugar, water and flavouring – is particularly famous in Sicily, and every town has its own favourite texture and prime flavouring. Sorbets are mostly made from water and fruit purée, and these too vary from town to town; flavours are usually sweet but now can often be savoury. A *semifreddo* (literally 'half frozen') is an ice cream with a higher content of fat or sugar, so that it does not set hard; a *spumoni* is a moulded dessert with an outer layer of ordinary ice cream and an interior of *semifreddo*. *Cassata* is a particular gelato speciality of Sicily; it uses the ingredients of a cake with the same name – marzipan, ricotta, dried fruit – as an ice cream. It once was a Christmas speciality, but can now be found all year round.

In any Sicilian *gelateria*, you can find flavours ranging from *fior di latte* or *panna* (literally cream), vanilla, lemon, pistachio, chocolate, hazelnut to *stracciatella* (vanilla with crunchy chocolate strands). The ranged containers look like bright, colourful jewels, and on summer evenings, customers cluster around, choosing the flavours to go in their cones or dishes, sometimes even three at one time!

ABOVE Ice creams and sorbets for sale in the old town of Taormina, on Sicily's south-east coast.

TOP LEFT A 19th-century engraving of sorbet sellers.

ABOVE LEFT An ice cream van in Taormina provides refreshment for tourists and locals alike.

Watermelon ice cream

Gelato di cocomoro

This is my very determined effort to emulate a true Sicilian classic. It's served throughout the island and devoured by young and old alike.

1 medium watermelon (you'll need 720 ml/24 fl. oz. watermelon purée)

200 ml/¾ cup milk

200 ml/¾ cup double/heavy cream

60 g/4 tablespoons caster/granulated sugar

1 teaspoon vodka (optional) – helps with the freezing, not for taste

2 tablespoons dark/bittersweet chocolate chips, to serve (optional)

Serves 4–6

Prepare the watermelon; remove the seeds and process the flesh in a food processor until you have the consistency of a purée.

Mix all the ingredients together, except the chocolate chips, and combine well.

Place in an ice-cream machine and churn, or alternatively freeze in a metal container and every 2 hours mix by hand. This should take 6–7 hours in total.

Serve with chocolate chips if desired. They look fun and mimic the watermelon seeds.

Lemon sorbet

Sorbetto di limone siciliano

330 g/1⅔ cups golden caster/granulated sugar

250 ml/1 cup lemon juice (i.e. juice of 10 lemons, organic for maximum flavour)

100 ml/7 tablespoons limoncello

6–8 lemon halves, hollowed out and frozen

Serves 6–8

Ubiquitous across Sicily and, quite simply, my all-time favourite. Serving it in a lemon makes it more elegant.

Stir the sugar and 375 ml/1½ cups of water in a medium saucepan over medium-high heat until the sugar dissolves. Bring to the boil and cook for 2 minutes. Cool completely – I do this a day in advance.

Add the lemon juice, limoncello and 250 ml/1 cup water to the sugar syrup. Stir to combine.

Freeze and churn in an ice-cream machine or freeze in a metal container and, after 2 hours, fork over to break up the ice crystals. Repeat every 2 hours until you have a fine sorbet texture.

Serve in frozen lemon halves, with a little lemon zest on top if you wish.

Sicilian lemonade syrup

Limonata

Making the most of their legendary lemons, this refreshing, fragrant drink is enjoyed all over the island with various treats. In my various attempts to concoct the right recipe, I have found this to be the best. I must say that I am not too keen on a very sweet lemonade – if you prefer a sweeter version, add another 50 g/3 tablespoons sugar.

250 g/1¼ cups golden caster/granulated sugar

200 ml/¾ cup water

10 whole basil leaves

grated zest of 5 lemons

freshly squeezed juice of 15 lemons (organic for maximum flavour)

Makes 350 ml/1½ cups

In a medium saucepan, mix the sugar and water together and set over gentle heat to dissolve the sugar. When the sugar has dissolved, add the basil leaves and leave to infuse until the sugar syrup is cold.

When the sugar syrup is cold, remove the basil. Add the lemon zest and juice. Mix well and store in the fridge. This recipe makes a citrusy syrup that can be mixed with sparkling/soda water for a perfect Sicilian lemonade or even used in cocktails.

Store in the fridge for 4 weeks, but it really won't last that long!

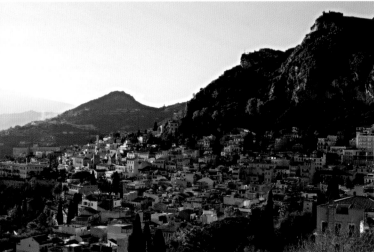

Candied peel

Candite

While researching this recipe, I came across literally hundreds and hundreds of recipes and variations. I asked family, friends and Sicilian relatives and I've ended up with this recipe, which works really well. Sicilian 'candite' is extremely diverse, with all sorts of fruits and flavours, including violets (violetti candite).

1 orange

1 lemon

1 grapefruit

350 g/1¾ cups caster/granulated sugar

1 vanilla pod/bean, split

1 star anise

1 cinnamon stick

Makes 200 g/1½ cups

Using a sharp knife, cut the orange into 4 wedges and remove the flesh. Cut each piece of peel into 3–4 chunky strips. Repeat with the lemon and grapefruit.

Place the peels into a saucepan, cover with cold water and bring to the boil. Simmer for 10 minutes and then drain. Repeat this process twice more (this process removes the bitterness), then drain the peels and set aside while you prepare the sugar syrup.

Tip the sugar into a heavy-bottomed pan and add 350 ml/1⅓ cups water. Add the vanilla, star anise and cinnamon. Place over medium heat to dissolve the sugar, stirring occasionally.

Add the peels to the pan and boil steadily for 40 minutes, stirring occasionally, until the peels become soft and translucent, and almost all of the syrup has been absorbed. Keep a close eye on the pan as it can burn.

Using tongs, remove the peels from the pan one at a time and lay on a sheet of parchment paper in a single layer. Cover and leave to dry overnight. They should no longer be sticky. Store in a box or airtight container for up to 1 month.

Chop and add to cakes, biscuits, cookies and desserts, as required.

Index

Picture credits

Acknowledgements

Creating this book began on the launch of my previous book, A Gourmet Guide to Oil and Vinegar. Cindy Richards, Publisher of Ryland Peters & Small, had just returned from a trip to Sicily and her eagerness for the subject mirrored mine. And so the quest to research and delve into this fascinating island began.

Thanks are also due to:

Editorial Director Julia Charles, who yet again inspired me to work hard and produce a book worthy of her keen and excellent eye and passion; my editor, Nathan Joyce, for all his steady reassurances and confidence; Gillian Haslam for seeing the book through to its final pages; and Remigio De Rienzo for checking my Italian spelling.

Photographer David Munns – the minute I met him, I knew my book was in safe hands; food stylist Emily Kydd for creating such beautiful food; and Victoria Allen for the gorgeous props used in the photographs to bring Sicilian food to life. Designer Toni Kay – gorgeous to have you working on this book. I love all you do.

Sally Daniels, my friend and such a professional, as deciphering my scribbles is quite, quite painful. She is super bright and utterly efficient and great fun too. Susan Fleming for her help, and Rachel Rowling also – fabulous friends and endless thanks for their generous support. Margaret Godfrey, for friendship and prayers and support and spirit.

Antonia, my darling little girl, for travelling to Sicily with me, eating non-stop and being brutally honest, in the way that only children can be, about all the dishes we tasted. I have the fondest memories of her running wild on Mondello Beach, full of delicious gelato.